'It feels long overdue to have a m

'It feels long overdue to have a m... ing. We are seeing mental health is: merging home and work lives coul(paradoxically less connected. Listen challenge, so this is an important b(– helpful not preachy, practical and .... by solid research and experience.'

Dr Sue Round, HRVP Talent, Diversity and Inclusion at BP

'This book is a transformational read that takes us far beyond what we often think listening is about, into essential areas of human communication, connection and understanding. The book is rich with storytelling, research and tips relevant to all of us in our personal and professional lives. The breadth of the writer's experience from the theatre to global business enables her to take us on a compelling journey to explore what's possible when we unlock the full power of listening.'

Cath Bishop, author of *The Long Win*

'In a world which demands us to constantly "shift" being a great listener really does matter now more than ever. By uniting both theory and practice, van Hool confidently brings the idea to life and offers practical steps to achieve this, whether in a one-on-one setting or in the context of a large organisation. All of us, coaches, teachers, leaders, parents, friends will benefit from the useful prompts offered.'

Dr Caroline Horner, i-coach academy

'This book is conversational, engaging, moving and above all really helpful. We all know the power of making fundamental shifts in how we think and what we do but making those shifts "stick", so they just become who we are, is another thing altogether. The writer's real examples of listening and being listened to are relevant and they resonate. Combine those with her practical tips, then you have a book that delivers – one you will go back to again and again over the years, and a book that you will definitely gift to others.'

Judith Batchelar OBE, Director of Corporate Responsibility, Sustainability & Public Affairs

'You cannot be heard as a leader if you do not learn to listen. This book teaches the fundamentals of both. An invaluable read for any manager who actively wants to become a more skilled listener and communicate more effectively.'

Chris Schulze-Melander, CEO Eat Real & Proper

'Not only a fascinating and easy read, but full of generous advice, broad examples and practical "shifts" that blend the art of communication with the gift of listening! I'd expect nothing less from Janie, who is a master of communication.'

Carol Welch, Managing Director, UK, Ireland & Commercial Officer Europe Odeon Cinemas Group

'There were points in Janie's book that pulled me up short and really made me question whether I was as good a listener as I thought I was.'

Alan Robertson, Business Psychologist and creator of VoicePrint™

'Leadership is about creating followers. Here is a powerful toolkit to understand the importance and techniques of making the shift to listening – deeply, at all levels – to establish connections and crafting relevant dialogue so that leaders can achieve engagement and are themselves "listened" to. Great job.'

Paul Griffith, Professor of Practice, Hult International Business School

'A practical guide essential to anyone making things happen in organisations. This is a topic that leaders overlook when pushing for improvements in how we work.'

Hamish Scott, Founder, Centre for Management Research in Action, Business school Professor and fractional strategy director

'The writer brings the insights from working with leaders in all kinds of organisations, debunks the myth that real leaders "give orders", demonstrates how listening underpins successful leaders at all levels – and provides the practical steps to get going.'

Keith Leslie, Chair of Samaritans, author of *A Question of Leadership*, former McKinsey and Deloitte partner

the listening shift

Transform your organization
by listening to your people
and helping your people
listen to you

JANIE VAN HOOL

First published in Great Britain by Practical Inspiration Publishing, 2021

ISBN   9781788602570 (print)
       9781788602563 (epub)
       9781788602556 (mobi)

Practical Inspiration
Publishing

.

For Russell, Tilly and Bella

It isn't what you have in your pocket that makes you thank-ful, but what you have in your heart.

Anon

Contents

Foreword

When you look out of a train window, the trees up close fly by in a blur, the fields in the middle distance glide past, and the far-off hills don't appear to move at all. Similarly, in public life: newspaper headlines fly by in a blur, political shifts glide past, and the natural world doesn't appear to move at all. Or so it was... until the climate crisis began to distort and accelerate environmental change. Today, it is as if when we look out of the train window, we can see the far-off hills gathering speed, shifting gear, and catching up with our train.

I was first introduced to Janie van Hool, shortly after being appointed the UK Commissioner to the Global Commission on Adaptation. Co-chaired by Ban ki-Moon, Kristalina Georgieva and Bill Gates, the Commission was set up to provide greater political visibility to the need to prepare for climate shocks – too much water, too little water, too hot, too cold and wildfires. This was a huge opportunity for me to showcase the work of the Environment Agency, which I chair, on the global stage, and shine a spotlight on the growing evidence that people all over the world, at every income level, are already being affected in one way or another by climate change. I needed to up my game as a communicator, experience my own shift, and Janie offered to help.

As we started to work together, it became abundantly clear how important it is to start with listening and this is the focus of Janie's wonderful book. She reveals how we are not taught how to listen, and that we need to address this before we can really engage with each other. How we need to be bolder about how we challenge ourselves to listen well. And that we need to communicate in a way that helps other people to listen to us. This is especially important where messages are hard to hear, and we need to find ways to help people engage.

I do hope the practical steps that Janie has set out in *The Listening Shift* are as helpful to you, as they have been to me, and become a resource that you can dip into time and time again. Janie is not only generous with her insight but also her emphasis on others and being kind. So, rather than issue a spoiler alert, I leave you with a quote from Jane Austen which captures for me the essence of Janie's advice: "Emma felt that she could not now show greater kindness than in listening."

Emma Howard Boyd
Chair, Environment Agency

Part One

This shift matters
The foundations and layers of listening

The first part of this book is all about listening. We'll look at why listening matters, how to prepare yourself to listen well, how to understand others and a process for listening that will help you to reflect upon and develop your skills.

Why shift?

Life is full of shifts – and these shifts are often huge changes arising from small decisions or brief moments.

To shift is to move absolutely from one point to another – a groundswell of energy that may bring insight and effect change, no matter how subtle or nuanced. It is definite.

A shift is also a unit of work – a commitment for a defined period of time. The insinuation is that a shift may be hard, and effort is involved. It may be repetitive, habitual, a commitment. The word 'shift' has Germanic origins – from *schichten*, which means to stratify or layer.

This book is just that: the layers needed to be an exceptional communicator lie in the foundations of skilful listening, all the way up to serving your listeners by helping them listen to you.

1

Get your shift together

Where we explore the foundations in this book, consider why listening well matters and start the process of reflecting on your own listening.

- How I came to write this book.
- The commercial case for listening – what's possible in your business when you develop a listening culture.
- What you will find in the chapters that follow.
- Why this shift matters – the listening landscape and how it affects the way we listen in work and society.
- Prompts to help you think about your own listening.

How I came to write this book

It is October half-term in 1977. I am 11 years old and spending the week with my mum and dad, auntie and uncle in Kent. This is a familiar picture. They are playing cards... I am reading. Except I'm not really... I am listening to a conversation that I have heard many times. They are reminiscing; there is laughter, outrage, wistfulness, disagreement. They are also engaged in a competitive card battle. There is an occasional slapping down of cards onto the table and a yelp of disbelief. They go back to their conversation and I zone in and out. There is a cat on the sofa beside me – much more interesting!

This is a picture of my childhood in the 1970s. I am an only child, and these moments forged my path of listening. I became adept at participating in conversations with adults that were significant learning experiences. By listening to adult exchanges, I learned a few things to avoid, planted a few ambitions and developed some of my own values by reflecting on the drama I witnessed being played out in the conversations around me. These were sometimes fascinating experiences, and sometimes very dull ones – normal family conversations. I am also privileged to have had the gift of being listened to – and that is a gift like no other.

I spent a good deal of time on my own... time that was filled with reading. I am an insatiable reader. Nothing helps us understand the perspective of others like a good book – the rare opportunity to find out what's really going on in someone's head as they navigate life. Reading is listening – learning to understand the perspective of others, while considering, reflecting and comparing world-views.

Time spent absorbed in the lives of others – fictional or biographical – drew me further into the exploration of people's motivations – so much so that I ended up studying acting at the Royal Academy of Dramatic Arts (RADA) in London. This was where I learned so much about the importance of listening in performance. Acting, as they say, is reacting. You have to be totally present and in the moment in order to be able to respond truthfully. I learned about the music of the voice and how to play it like an instrument to inform, to inspire, to create mood. I learned how to breathe, how to project confidence, how to manage stage fright. I learned to use my physicality as a way of creating characters and influencing audiences. I learned how to master physical presence. I didn't realize it then, but all that skill in performing is essentially a great big exercise in listening. It's an immutable truth that a great performer is as much an exceptional listener as they are an exceptional speaker – but their skill starts with listening.

After 12 years, and with two small children, I decided to move on from acting. I studied for a Master's degree in voice studies and started to teach. The study of voice is essentially the study of listening – paying attention to small changes that might be made to take a voice from flat to engaging, from soft to confident, from 'strongly accented' to 'easy to understand' and more besides. This was an exercise in detailed, precise listening with a high probability of solving problems and enabling transformation. Wonderful!

As I was writing my dissertation, I took an 'out-of-the-blue' opportunity to use my skills to shape and support a leadership team with their communication. I loved it and have now worked in this field for over 20 years. I have spent thousands of hours listening to understand the context of a leader's situation, experimenting with techniques and listening to their responses. I have listened to diagnose, solve, shift and support. I have found ways to help leaders inspire with strategy, vision and storytelling. I have built influencing models, created conversation frameworks, supported interview preparation and created impactful conference communication. I have certainly listened – but I've also seen the power of leadership listening and the transformational effect this has on organizations and on the engagement of the people involved. The listener–speaker exchange can – and should – be magic.

Then, aged 50, I learned *just* to listen. I trained as a listening volunteer with Samaritans – a UK charity dedicated to listening to people in distress whose mission is to reduce the number of suicides by offering to simply listen... not to solve, give advice or offer a perspective, but rather to give another person the time and space to explore what is going on for them. Oh yes, I've been listening all my life, but the Samaritans' approach to listening is where I learned what's possible – what the transformational power of being heard offers. This has had the most profound impact on me as I open my eyes to the challenges we face in society.

I have realized that we are not really taught how to listen – circumstances may create the right conditions for some more than others, but essentially we are left to our own devices. And yet I have learnt that being listened to can literally save a life.

Writing this book gave me the opportunity to reflect on the immeasurable value of skilful communication in transforming individuals, businesses and society. The book contains ideas, practice suggestions, strategies, stories and much more.

If, on reading it, you have thoughts, learning, experiences or advice that you'd like to share, then I would love to listen. Contact me at Janie@listeningshift.com.

Why do any of this shift?
The commercial case for listening and helping others listen to you

The greatest value any leader can offer an organization is the ability to create the conditions that will enable people to be at their best.

Businesses need leaders who build winning teams that can outperform their competition; leaders who demonstrate competence and integrity; leaders who are able to identify a shared purpose that people believe in; leaders who work tirelessly to create a culture where people feel included and respected. Leaders who are driven by the question, 'How can I make you more successful?'

In other words, businesses need emotionally intelligent leaders who have a competitive mindset with a compassionate heart.

Recent events have expedited a shift in where and how we work – a blend of office-based and remote-working beckons and challenges us all. As technology advances, replacing many jobs and making us rely increasingly on connecting with each other through virtual platforms, the importance of leaders who are able to connect and to understand their colleagues' perspectives, hopes and fears can't be overstated.

Leaders must develop exceptional communication skills and continue to prioritize and grow them. An ability to ask the right questions and listen – deeply – to the answers is not a 'nice to have' mindset – it's the only way to be successful.

As Marcus Buckingham said in his book *First, Break All the Rules*,[1] 'People leave managers, not companies.' A failure to help people feel valued, appreciated and understood – seen and heard – has a negative impact on culture, affecting business growth and reputation.

> *The great myth of our times is that technology is communication. It puts up a great barrier between human beings leaving us yearning for intimacy.*
>
> **Libby Larsen**

Your people need a good listening to

The quality of your listening determines the quality of the other person's speaking… and vice versa.

In other words, if you listen well, you are setting another person up for success and if you speak well, you are ensuring your listener will be able to listen well. Whether you are listening remotely, or in a room with someone, this is a guiding principle for successful communication.

Listening well reduces fear and resistance to change. It minimizes gossip and the spread of uncertainty. It humanizes leadership, allowing people to connect through shared values and understanding. It builds communities by fostering an environment of trust, increasing collaboration and a stronger commitment to teams.

Listening well brings customers to your door and keeps them on your side.

---

[1] Marcus Buckingham, *First, Break All the Rules*, 2005.

Listening well is not agreeing, advising or colluding. It's not waiting to speak, filling time or a planning opportunity. It's not about nodding your head, uttering sounds of agreement or concentrating on matching body language. It's an art, a skill, a practice, a commitment. It requires preparation, self-awareness and self-control. It demands curiosity, patience, generosity and a desire to understand... then, it becomes a gift received, reciprocated and rewarded.

A listening culture where people listen and feel listened to will make your business more successful – and who wouldn't want that?

What you will find in this book

In **Part 1**, we think about listening as a broad concept and explore why it matters so much to us at work, at home and in society generally. We also consider why we don't focus on it more as a taught or learned skill.

Chapter 2: Shift work explores possible routes to implementing a program of listening across your organization that will show your people and communities you are serious about developing a listening culture. We'll look at options available to you and consider how to change the way your people communicate in meetings.

Chapter 3: I've got shift to do – managing your impact begins with learning to listen to yourself. The widely quoted metaphor of self-care is being asked to put on your own oxygen mask before helping others put on theirs during the safety briefing on a plane, and it applies here. How can you listen effectively to other people – manage the noise of distraction – if you haven't managed to master it in listening to yourself?

We then explore why empathy is helpful. Listening to and understanding yourself will pave the way to develop a finely tuned ability to empathize with others. The act of listening enables empathy, so we explore how you can work at being empathetic... and continue to improve.

Our approach to listening well needs to start with technique and I include 10 steps to listening well here not to make the act of listening mechanical, but because sometimes, with some people and in some situations, following a disciplined structure allows us to stay present and do the work – technique allows us to put in a good shift.

The first part of the book closes with crossing the bridge between listening and speaking, which is to consider the importance of setting an intention. Intention is gold in an important conversation or presentation. Setting a tone that listeners can feel – whether speaking or listening – allows the other person to be present, clear and focused. An intention to listen allows the speaker to play their part well. An intention to speak well allows the listener to listen. This is an exchange that serves everybody well.

In *Part 2,* we consider how to help others listen to you. After all, they are giving you their time and attention, so it's vital that you find the right ways to make it easy for them to do so.

Chapter 4: This shift means something focuses on relevance in helping others listen. We communicate because we want to say something. We have information that needs disseminating, and we write it, say it or present it to our listeners. We know listening is hard, yet we expect people to tune in and remember it all – hanging on our every word. But what if it isn't relevant to them? Why would they listen to that? In this section, we'll explore three useful tools for creating relevance for your listeners: giving listeners a reason to listen; engaging them with carefully chosen metaphors;

and learning to tell *their* stories to engage and inspire with content that is meaningful to *them*.

Struggle is compelling – it is right at the heart of every unfolding drama. In *Chapter 5: This shift is hard – show the struggle*, we'll look at the power of sharing your struggle and how it relates to relevance. Overcoming obstacles is dynamite in helping others to sit up and listen. Your stories, personal experiences and insights gained over the course of your life are a compelling way of connecting with others and a cast-iron guarantee that they will understand what you want them to do – and remember it. We will look at the options for sharing your own experiences in a powerful way.

Finally, with all the heart of a dragon slayer, you'll still need a strong toolkit of technique to carry you through. *Chapter 6: You've got this shift – the importance of technique in helping others listen* provides this. It shows how important it is to understand the skill of being succinct, the security and freedom offered to the speaker by structure in planning presentations and conversations, the power of using your voice effectively and the relevance of setting and environment. These are all transformative when it comes to helping us listen.

The book concludes with a reminder that building and maintaining our relationships – no matter who they are with – is a sustained and dedicated act of generosity and kindness. *Chapter 7: Shift happens – how to take care of yourself as a communicator* offers suggestions that I hope you will take to heart and use to keep you on track. I'll leave you with a lesson learned by me… I hope it reminds us all of the purpose of listening to others.

The listeners: Helping us listen

In the process of researching for *The Listening Shift*, I interviewed a number of people whose expertise depends on listening well, or on helping people to listen. Summaries of each of their individual perspectives, along with any advice they chose to give, are scattered throughout the book.

Extra resources as you read

Reading is a form of listening. The words on the page offer us an insight into the writer's thoughts, motivations, beliefs, heartfelt joys and frustrations. We can't interrogate their thinking – only witness it. If we disagree, we must read on – or walk away. If we agree, we may enjoy the next chapter with enthusiasm. We pay attention as we read. We begin to understand and reflect on what we learn. Reading is a great way to learn how to be empathetic as we are blessed to understand the full picture of the protagonist's story and how it affects them – something we rarely experience in our lives.

How you read may give you a little insight into how you listen… what are the conditions you need to be able to really get into the narrative? What time of day works best for your concentration? Do you 'binge' or 'bitesize'? What do you find easy to read – long, narrative flowing passages or short paragraphs with space on the page? What do you like? What annoys you? Perhaps you can use this book to reflect on how reading works best for you… and consider what this tells you about how you listen in conversation. One size never fits all, but this first, gentle reflection is a positive place to start. There are no rules, just noticing.

But reading, while interesting, helpful and informative, is not the best way to bring listening and speaking to life. I wanted to offer you the chance to listen to real examples of conversations and presentations, to be stimulated by sound and music, to be moved by poetry, to experience a range of meditations. To that end, I have compiled a series of listening experiences for you to access to stimulate your listening as you read on. You'll also find links to further reading, viewing and how to contact me at www.listeningshift.com if you'd like to explore further.

A word of warning

I am aware that we buy books like this one in the hope that the pages contain the answers we need to be able to repro-gramme ourselves and become masters of the subject. I hope to be able to absorb the information from many of the books I buy through just having them on my bookshelf, or in my bag. Of course, it doesn't work like that and I can't offer you a panacea or cast a spell to make it happen. But I do have some good news… Being a great listener is not magic, or even talent – it involves self-awareness, discipline and generosity. This is something we can *all* do, and many of the suggestions here will help you transform your skills… If you are willing to do the work.

My own research backs up the insights offered by others over many years – we all think we are pretty good listeners, and we all feel other people don't listen very well. This dissonance is the heart of the problem.

If we start from the premise that we could be better, we will be able to honestly appraise our listening and take action where needed.

Challenge your view of yourself as you read this book. None of us is a perfect listener. It's hard, as we will see, but it's rewarding. Accept that you have work to do and take it on. If you commit to improving even one listening relationship in your life, you will have done something amazing.

When you talk, you are only repeating what you already know, but if you listen you may learn something new.

Dalai Lama

Why this shift matters
The listening landscape

'Listen!'…

Command, direction, request or plea, we've all heard it. A single word announcing a need for the full, undivided attention of those present. For practical and emotional reasons, in crisis situations, building relationships and whenever we want to find out what is going on, we need to be heard – and we need to be able to listen well.

We are social creatures, constantly involved in communication during our waking hours – whether writing, reading, speaking or listening, we are engaging with others to learn, understand and progress our conversations.

If it matters so much, then we need to be exceptionally good at it.

In his book *Outliers,*[2] Malcolm Gladwell tells us that to become an expert in something takes 10,000 hours of working at it. On that basis, to be an expert as a communicator, at eight hours a day, five days a week, would mean around five years; at two hours a day of constant focus on the subject, you're looking at more than 19 years.

You might sit back at this point and feel that you've passed the test, made it – spent the necessary time. Of course, Gladwell's thesis is that to achieve expertise, we must work

---

[2] Malcolm Gladwell, *Outliers,* 2009.

diligently and be constantly improving. There is dedication involved – effort. In some of the examples he uses, we might even say obsession.

We may all have a long way to go as we strive to be expert communicators.

Listening falls into the category of 'soft skills' in personal development. This undervalues the commitment involved in the necessary learning. Any expert in their field of performance will tell you that mastery involves practice, coaching and asking for help or feedback from a team of supportive, trusted advisors. It can't be done in a 45-minute webinar, a half-day workshop or as a module on a development programme.

I have noticed during my years of working in leadership development that the commitment to becoming an expert communicator is easily diverted to learning new skills – what's next, what's different, what will set the leader apart and make them successful in growing their business and leaving a legacy. Listening remains important to them, but stating an intention to listen doesn't make it happen well. To do that, you need to put in the hard hours.

We must continue to build excellence in the foundations of communication and view getting better at it as a lifelong practice of learning, testing and reviewing our development.

To become an exceptional communicator, I urge you to start with listening well, then think about how to help people listen to you.

Why is listening so hard?

Who taught you to listen? If you are lucky, you will have grown up with great role models and been listened to as a child, learning by experience and being guided towards what works and what doesn't. Perhaps your education gave you the skill to listen and speak with appropriate focus... but probably not. Most of us are not taught how to listen – just told to do it. The International Listening Association,[3] a US not-for-profit organization set up to advance the practice, teaching and research of listening globally, claims that only 2% of people have had formal education in listening, whereas education in speaking is ubiquitous and oral communication skills turn up in the top 10 requirements in recruiter surveys over and over again.

There are psychological barriers to our ability to listen well, too. In 1957, psychologist Leon Festinger[4] wrote about cognitive dissonance and its effect on our decision-making, beliefs and behaviours. Dissonance is a process in which we find ways to justify our thoughts because to challenge them would be too uncomfortable. This is particularly pertinent if the dissonance experienced is about our self-concept – that is, if we believe ourselves to be kind and empathetic listeners and then have that challenged by someone or something, we will need to find a way to dismiss or reduce the challenger.

I have a client experience that illustrates this well (see box below).

> 'A' – a senior leader in a global organization – is the only woman in a team of six men who are also senior leaders in the business. She is not the most senior person in the team and meetings are often chaired by her boss. She regularly experiences her contributions

---

[3] See www.listen.org.
[4] Leon Festinger, *A Theory of Cognitive Dissonance*, 1957.

in these meetings being overlooked or ignored by her colleagues. She finds this frustrating and demotivating, although she recognizes that 'this happens'.

Recording one of these meetings and playing it back to her boss results in a classic case of cognitive dissonance in action. Her boss responds with two protests:

1. 'We absolutely want to hear from "A", but she needs to speak up more! It's as if she doesn't want to contribute.'
2. 'The focus of this meeting wasn't about "A's" area – she didn't really need to say anything on this occasion. We would normally involve her much more.'

There are so many examples of this at play in our daily interactions, and I can understand why 'A's' boss was trying to explain and justify the group's behaviour. To have owned the evidence would have caused enormous discomfort and challenged him to think deeply about how he leads and how he interacts in meetings with female colleagues. In listening, he would have caused himself distress. It's not surprising that he would seek to avoid it.

In time, 'A' goes on to leave the organization, citing meeting behaviour as a major cause of frustration and upset. I believe that had her boss listened differently, she might still be there and adding enormous value to the business.

Barriers to listening well are not just psychological – you may be tired, cold, distracted. You may have backache, be home-schooling children, you may be feeling sad, worried, under pressure or a host of other emotions, some of which may be positive. Distractions come in all forms, shapes and sizes. They make listening hard and, as we will see in this book, they may be overcome – but it isn't always easy to make that happen.

Cultural influences on listening

If learning to listen well is not automatically taught to families and in education, and there are complex emotional and psychological factors that increase our resistance to mastering the skills, it's concerning to recognize the lack of good listening in our wider society.

We have become a society that talks – a lot. Some 720,000 hours of video content is uploaded to YouTube each day. Algorithms tell us that the average visit lasts for 40 minutes, or that we spend on average a total of 2.5 hours on social media every day.

Social media has become a huge part of the way we communicate, encouraging us to put our lives online, curating and narrating a constructed version of how we live and insisting that others pay attention to us.

In 2020, following the tragic death of the presenter Caroline Flack, hundreds of messages appeared all over social media urging us to #bekind and calling for people to listen to each other with compassion. This recognition of the impact of messages broadcast on social media struck a powerful chord, but it doesn't seem to have changed anything on the listening front. Voices insisting that we should listen may still be found seizing the narrative but talking remains the order of the day.

Later in 2020, protest movements sprung up in the United States and the United Kingdom highlighting huge injustices facing black and indigenous people, and people of colour (BIPOC) in both countries. Powerful voices called for change and a healthy dialogue began. It seemed that we had reached a pivotal moment when we might be ready to engage with real change, where those affected felt able to speak up and share their experiences, and where protagonists were ready to acknowledge their individual part in causing harm. Yet there still seems to be more talking than listening, more defensiveness than understanding – and consequently more harm still being done.

Part of this is down to our political system. All political parties are keen to be seen as listeners. William Hague spoke about it at the Conservative Party Conference in 1998, Tony Blair in 2000, Nigel Farage when campaigning for a BREXIT referendum and David Cameron after losing it. Jeremy Corbyn used listening as a pillar of his leadership; Keir Starmer in 2020 claimed to have been 'listening and asking for conversations with people that are difficult rather than easy' and, on winning his party's leadership election in the summer of 2020, Ed Davey said that, following three successive election defeats, his party must 'start listening'. Of course, these are mostly platitudes, intended to project the speaker as a good person, a change-maker, someone worthy of trust. The problem arises with their style of listening and the skill they have in doing it well.

In politics, an intention to listen is usually a cover for the opportunity to talk. Listening is explaining, denying, changing the subject.

Political listening is similar to the issues faced by listening in businesses – the listening is likely to be selective. There's an element of the echo chamber in who is involved in the debate. The domain of conversation lies with people whose preoccupation may likely be with power and hierarchy, whose voices express themselves through advocacy, direction and controlling the narrative. The debate doesn't feel relevant to listening audiences and they are reluctant to give their time and attention to it.

In *The Politics of Listening*,[5] Leah Bassel questions the political attitudes that allow certain voices to be silenced or ignored. Speaking at the Diversity and the City event in 2018, she said, 'Listening to the experience of diverse employees requires that we are willing to change roles of speaking and listening – requires that we stop talking.'[6]

Politicians and business leaders must value listening differently and role-model the change they make so we may all see it and learn from it. Our political leaders must pay attention to different voices and listen without defending. If the conversations we see played out in front of us, moderated by a journalist or interviewer, are simply an exchange of point and counterpoint, then we will all stop listening – if, indeed, we haven't already.

---

[5] Leah Bassel, *The Politics of Listening*, 2017.
[6] Leah Bassel, *Diversity and the City, and the Politics of Listening*, February 2018. Available from www.youtube.com/watch?v= QGzj1jl_MRM [accessed 6 February 2021].

Why does listening matter so much now?

There are immediate priorities calling for all of us to listen at the moment:

1. *The need for conversations about diversity.* These are painful conversations whichever way you look at it – those who feel harmed, and those who seek to acknowledge playing their part in having done harm (however unintentional that was) want to speak out. Deep listening is needed, without justification. It is time to approach the conversations as partners, with concrete commitments to making change. Any hint of assumption, judgement or minimizing what is being said will damage the relationship further, so it is essential to manage these conversations with skilful listening.

   A business needs diversity of thought to be successful. There is a powerful business case for conversations about diversity to be immediately prioritized, but they will not be successful without first acknowledging the need for, and developing the skills of, a listening culture to support the conversations.

2. *Inclusion.* As social creatures, people need to feel connected to others. Connection promotes wellbeing and enhances psychological safety. Listening with empathy, compassion and generosity makes people feel cared about – they matter. Engagement surveys often flag requests for improved communication and, in response, employees are flooded with more emails,

newsletters, information updates and blogs from the leadership team. This might be interesting content to read, but is it addressing the wrong question? Concerns about communication are usually a red flag – a sign that people are feeling disconnected, uncertain, excluded. Listening to the concerns expressed by your followers, again without defensiveness or justification, will start to build a bridge and signal a commitment to inclusivity as a priority.

3. *Enabling people to talk about mental health.* I have seen most of my client organizations make commitments to supporting mental health in the workplace, encouraging people to feel able to speak about their emotional experience, making it completely fine to be honest about challenges, difficulties and struggles, and validating their right to support. If we are expecting people to make this courageous step, we have to make sure that their speaking up is met with being listened to well. Anyone running a wellbeing programme in the workplace needs to have the right training and support to feel completely confident in their listening skills… and to know how to handle what they hear.

It's easy to miss suffering over technology, so your listening skills need even greater honing to be sure of paying attention to the right signals so you can be present for your people when they need you.

Prompts to help you think about your own listening

1. What's the purpose of listening?
2. Who taught you to listen well? How?
3. How do you make yourself easy to listen to?

The listeners: The doctor

Dr Rachel Mason is a junior doctor in the obstetrics and gynaecology department at Kingston Hospital. She describes listening as the foundation of her job.

She told me how vital it is that a patient feels heard – because feeling heard allows the patient to feel confident. It's an important route to building trust and, as a young, female doctor, this is a priority in being able to get a patient to paint a full picture of their situation.

Rachel tells me that in a typical 10-minute conversation, patients will tell you everything they think is important but that her role is to listen for the tiny details they may skim over, which may be very relevant to a diagnosis. Switching off – even momentarily – could mean missing something significant.

Fortunately, her medical degree placed great importance on communication. There was a constant emphasis on the value of, and skills involved in, listening along with an understanding of how to communicate clearly to people who are often in highly emotional states. Rachel feels this constant focus on communicating the right information in a clear, concise way, chunking complex details down and speaking in a carefully paced tone, has become second nature to her. She feels the time invested in this learning has benefited her personally, too, allowing her to develop a quality of attention that enhances all her relationships.

As a doctor, Rachel has learned to leave all preconceptions at the door – to suspend judgement about the way a patient may be behaving – because her observation is that fear or heightened emotion can make people behave rudely or be abusive. She takes a deep breath, reminds them that she is there to help and lets them speak. Then, she says, they turn a corner.

She shared that the pressure she experiences in her role is palpable – and that when she feels she's about to explode, she pauses for a moment, takes a breath and gathers herself. It's an important process to allow her to give her best for her next patient.

Her advice inspired me. She intentionally prioritizes thanking others – expressing gratitude as much as she can. This, she says, boosts confidence – it creates a 'nicer environment'.

The hardest thing about her job is 'taking it home', sometimes wondering whether she made the right decisions. But she says that 'if she feels she treated people with respect and gratitude, then she knows she has done a good job'.

2

Shift work

Where we consider listening to different voices across your organization and explore a model that will help your listeners feel heard, whatever the conversation.

Shift work can be tough and involves work that often falls outside standard working schedules. I use the term here because your 'listening shifts' may feel like an extra load and involve planning time that is additional to your role.

I believe your efforts will be rewarded.

- Five ways to listen across your organization.
- How to run a listening meeting.
- The speaker/listener technique.

Five ways to listen across your organization

In 2017, Henry Ward, the CEO of equity management plat-form Carta, published his company's shadow organizational chart on the Carta.com website.[1]

Ward's traditional hierarchical organizational chart is like any other – a top-down 'family tree'. But his shadow chart is a detailed network created to show the complex web of influencing relationships that exist in the Carta organization. Ward wanted to find out who the influencers were in his business and how they affected culture and decision-making relative to their position in the company.

The results are interesting – not least because when Ward investigated who the top 20 influencers in his company were, he was humbled to discover that as CEO he did not even make the top 10.

I doubt that he's alone.

Listening is an influencing opportunity across your orga-nization – but it needs to be continuous, always on... and genuine.

---

[1] Henry Ward, *The Shadow Organizational Chart*, Henry Ward Blog, September 2018. Available from https://carta.com/blog/the-shadow-organizational-chart [accessed 8 February 2021].

The following are some ways to get listening in your business:

1. *Try a listening audit.* No one has time to complete lengthy engagement surveys. The purpose of engaging should be to start a conversation – to open up debate rather than provide data that is put into action plans. Use the opportunity to create dialogue by asking questions that will help you to understand how you can serve your people better as a communicator. Think carefully about the questions that are most appropriate to your business and how you work together as a community. Here are some suggestions for you to test out:
   • Do you feel listened to by the people who matter to you at work?
   • What makes you feel heard?
   • How could we listen better as an organization?

2. *Find your listeners – and train them well.* This should not just be a human resources (HR) responsibility or project. Certainly, anyone in your business who is expected to chair meetings needs to be a well-trained listener, but you can go much further than that. Promote the initiative as a culture-change programme, state its importance and then find out who is genuinely curious about listening to the views of colleagues. These may be people from anywhere in the business, and ideally should be representative of every part of the business. Once you have your pool of curious, compassionate listeners, make sure they are taught to listen exceptionally well. This will

need more than a one-off workshop on the subject. I advise a specialist programme designed for your organization using blended learning – online and face-to-face learning sessions supported by tools and peer support groups. Celebrate the contribution of your listeners – hold them up as examples of excellence in your business culture, publicly acknowledging and appreciating what they do. If, as a leader, you are seen to value these skills highly, you will create a positive ripple effect.

3. *Start listening groups run by your listeners.* The principle of listening groups is similar to creating a focus group – a small sample of your population sharing their thoughts about particular topics or aspects of the business. The difference is that the intention has to be to listen fully and regularly. In community projects, such groups might be called 'listening circles'. The name matters, so choose something that is appropriate for your culture. The purpose of these groups is not output – you aren't seeking to solve a problem, or even diagnose one. It's a system of allowing people to share their experiences and to have them acknowledged by others in listening mode only. The sharing of stories is a system by which we have built relationships and communities for generations. Many of our current methods of communicating in soundbites are starving us of this connected practice and we need to bring it back.

4. *Hold 'town halls' or all-hands meetings.* This is an opportunity to really listen and respond to a large

number of people in your business. I have seen these events run as open Q&As, which can be successful, but you're relying on a few big personalities to speak up on behalf of others. This is a useful format to combine all the skills discussed in this book because you'll need to communicate clearly, simply and confidently, and respond openly with curiosity and an intent to build relationships.

Using some of the strategies in the second part of this book will help you frame your message so it can be heard, but how can you ensure interaction? Here are some of my favourite tactics:

- Ask for questions beforehand and respond to them. The audience at BBC's *Question Time* are asked to write down and submit their questions as they wait to take their seat in the audience before recording of the programme begins. These are then themed by producers. The best-framed question on the theme is the one posed. Taking this approach to asking questions before your meeting will give you a good idea of the most pressing and popular issues on people's minds.
- Allow time in the session to put people into small groups for 10 to 15 minutes of conversation – approximately five or six people per group. Give them a theme to discuss related to your message and ask them to come up with one question per group, which should be submitted either in writing or asked in plenary by a nominated spokesperson.

- Following a short presentation of issues or ideas, have the room separate into small groups, as above, but facilitated by one of your team (better still, one of your listeners). This needs to be a longer conversation – 30 minutes or so. Have a note-taker in each group submit findings, which may be done anonymously. Be crystal clear about why you are having someone take notes and how the notes will be used. Contributors will need to feel safe to speak up, otherwise you'll get polite commentary but nothing of real value.

- Create the conditions for people to interact creatively – public writing or recording areas where ideas may be shared in response to what has been heard. Sometimes called 'world cafés', these energizing routes to involving everyone in the conversation are powerful. Commit to summarizing what you read/hear and responding in the coming days. You can find out how to run a world café exercise by visiting the resources section at www.listeningshift.com. It will be important that you are visibly keeping your word as you engage in these conversations with a large number of people. Ensure you respond in a consistent way – if you aim to respond on Thursdays at 6.00 p.m. then that's when you must respond. No excuses. One of the most important criteria for influencing success, according to David Rock of the Neuroleadership Institute,[2] is

---

[2] David Rock, 'SCARF: A brain-based model for collaborating with others', in *Neuroleadership Journal*, June 2008, www.neuroleadership.com.

giving people certainty. This is often what people crave when they ask for better communication, according to Rock's research. You don't have to over-promise... certainty in this context means doing what you say you are going to do when you say you're going to do it.

5. *Conduct a listening roadshow or tour.* The senior leaders in your business – including the chair, the board and the non-executive directors – will benefit from regularly travelling to meet people across the business in person or connecting virtually to find out how people are feeling and to hear their ideas for positive and constructive change. This can be intimidating for people in the business who may be influenced by the status of those leading the conversation, so it's important to take the time to build trust by being open, honest and personal. The tone needs to feel sincere and meaningful – not staged in any way. Performance psychologist Charlie Unwin has a distinguished career – including as an army platoon commander in Iraq. I remember him talking about this role and referencing what he described as a three-quarter brew model of conversation. He would regularly meet with his troops and have a cup of tea with them, with the intention of finding out how they were really feeling. He said that you never really got to the truth of how they were until you were three-quarters of the way through the cup... then the conversation would move from polite to honest. It's vital to remember this during a listening tour – polite and stage-managed is often the approach to

communicating with senior leaders in any business. If you show patience and have the time to chew things over with people, about three-quarters of the way through a cup of tea you will get to the heart of things.

How to run a listening meeting

Meetings are a time-consuming and unavoidable feature of our working lives. If they work well, they enable understanding and productivity, and foster great team rapport. Nonetheless, meetings suffer from a bad reputation – there are countless articles on the frustrations associated with time taken up by meetings and the preparation necessary for them.

Listening in groups is the biggest listening challenge of all, owing to interpersonal dynamics, preferences in communication style and situational politics. It's easy to assume that others are listening and easy for us to appear to be listening when our thoughts may be elsewhere.

A client recently reported to me that during the first COVID-19 pandemic lockdown, the CEO called a three-day meeting with 40 people involved in each session. The agenda was issued at the beginning of the meeting as a presentation and the group was kept in plenary for the duration with only a lunch break each day.

At the end of the meeting each day, a long list of action points was issued. My client reported having 'no idea what they were supposed to do next'. During the meeting, most people were on mute and some kept their cameras on, but most did not. Everyone continued with their emails and other tasks.

In a highly sophisticated, globally successful company, such meeting behaviours are disappointingly still in evidence and they don't achieve the intended results. Instead, they lead to frustration, exhaustion and, inevitably, multitasking on a grand scale. No one is really listening.

Humans seem able to maintain focused attention for a matter of minutes before productivity declines, but with Outlook calendar invites, MS Teams and Zoom setting the timing for us at a full hour, or maybe 30 minutes, it's hard to walk away when we feel we're done with the conversation.

Creating the conditions for a listening meeting

1. Find out how long people would like meetings to run for… and how much time they would appreciate in between meetings to reflect and reset.
2. Solicit agenda agreement prior to meetings – find out what people want to discuss and what contributions they hope to make.
3. In the spirit of collaboration, make it possible to agree when, where and how the meeting could work best for them.

4. Aim for a meeting lasting only 15 minutes, then ask everyone to head off and consider the points or issues that have been raised. Alan Robertson of TalkWise Ltd[3] suggests reframing agenda points as issues rather than topics as a way of specifically engaging in a solutions-focused outcome.

5. Have people contribute to a shared document to continue the conversation in between meetings – for example, using Slack or Mural or another app-based platform that works for your business.

6. Reconvene with the information at an agreed date for another brief meeting to agree next steps. If it's about making a decision, you now have everyone's views and can then take an informal vote to see where the consensus lies.

Clarity, brevity and collaboration are essential to the set-up, but listening behaviour in a well-constructed meeting also matters.

---

[3] Alan Robertson, 'How to set better agendas'. Available from blogpost https://talk-wise.com/how-to-set-better-agendas [accessed 8 February 2021].

The speaker/listener technique

As you lead the way in listening meetings, you may want to try out a useful technique called the 'speaker/listener' technique. This technique emerged in couples therapy,[4] but it can easily and effectively be adapted to serve meeting conversations where listening skills need improving.

The technique is designed to allow the listener to focus on exactly what the other person is saying and to ensure that they demonstrate understanding. Neither person talks for too long. Each person is respectful of the other's right to say what they need to say. This avoids the 'now you, now me' approach to speaking in meetings where we endure a colleague speaking until we can get back to expressing our own view. I've seen this style of meeting conversation a lot… it's not listening; it's waiting, and it leads to interruption, interpretation and inference.

When trying out any new approach in communication, it is important to bear in mind that it might feel a bit laboured, effortful or clunky at first. Even if our usual approaches aren't 100% successful, chances are they will feel fluent and easily accessible thanks to years of use. Trying out a new approach may seem clumsy and unnatural, but it's worth pursuing because that's how the new habit will be formed. Acknowledging to

---

[4] Howard Markman et al., *Fighting for Your Marriage*, 2001.

everyone present that this is how it may feel and reviewing how it landed after the meeting will allow you all to continue to develop the method and strengthen your skill – along with uplifting the meeting behaviour. It's definitely worth a try!

Many years ago, I would spend my Friday evenings with a group of friends. We would go to the cinema and then have a curry afterwards – always to the same restaurant, where we would squeeze around a large round table and chat about the film, political issues, our lives and so on. Sometimes the conversations would become very heated and, without being aware of this technique, we naturally established a rule that whoever was holding the pepper pot (I know!) would be given the attention of the group and then, when they'd made their point, they would pass it on. We would set this up whenever exchanges started to get lively. It sometimes led to people trying to grab the pepper pot to have their say and, while it might sound a bit odd, it was actually a funny and generous way of including everyone. It made conversations more appropriate for a restaurant, which was a benefit, but it was surprisingly strengthening as a group, allowing us to understand different perspectives and trusting that we would have the opportunity to share our view if we wanted to. Some people were naturally more facilitative than others, and they would consciously include the quieter voices. It taught me a lot and I've used it in group facilitation with clients (not with a pepper pot, obviously, but with something useful from the meeting table).

Being heard is energizing – if you find this technique tricky to master, stick with it. The important thing is to know how others are feeling and if that yields the results you want, then you're onto a good thing. You could even try it with your friends and family!

The speaker/listener technique

Rules for the speaker:

1. Speak for yourself – don't mind read.
2. Don't go on and on.
3. Stop often to allow the listener to paraphrase.

Rules for the listener:

1. Paraphrase what you hear – don't interpret.
2. Don't interrupt or contradict – focus on what the speaker is saying.

Rules for both:

1. The speaker has the floor.
2. The speaker has the floor when the listener is paraphrasing.
3. Take turns being the speaker to ensure voices are heard equally.

What does that all mean?

Rules for the speaker

1. *Speak for yourself – don't mind read.* This is an important piece of self-awareness and control. It's tempting to hear someone express a thought and for us to guess what they mean, rather than clarifying. For example:

> *Speaker says:* 'This project has taken a lot of time and we need to step up our resources to get to the final stage.'
>
> *Listener mind reads:* 'They're going to ask me to work weekends.'

2. *Don't go on and on.* Have you ever seen the acronym WAIT? It stands for 'Why Am I Talking?' and is a useful check-in as we speak. Pay attention in your meetings to the length of time people take to express their views and see whether you can gauge what works best. I gave some feedback recently to a client I observed in a webinar conversation. He took a full four minutes to answer each question posed by the interviewer. His intention was to be helpful – setting context, offering a range of ideas and perspectives, and sharing his own experiences. However, this is way too long to expect anyone to be able to pay attention to a single point, making it impossible to paraphrase – and, therefore difficult to listen to.

3. *Stop often to allow the listener to paraphrase.* This one is tricky unless it's established as a process at the start of the meeting. You may only need to do it when subjects are complex, potentially inflammatory or painful to engage with. If it's not established as a device at the start of the conversation and you use it a lot, it can sound patronizing. Clarity of intention is key.

Rules for the listener

1. *Paraphrase what you hear – don't interpret.* Paraphrasing is the method of playing back a short

summary of the key points you've heard without interpreting them. The speaker should pause to allow you to do so.

An example of interpreting might be:

Speaker says: 'This project has taken a lot of time and we need to step up our resources to get to the final stage.'

Listener interprets: 'You think we haven't been working hard enough on the project and now you want to get more senior people in to finish it.'

Although the speaker's sentence is rather short to paraphrase (you could restate the whole sentence), an example of paraphrasing it could be:

Listener paraphrases: 'You're saying we need to throw everything at finishing.'

2. *Don't interrupt or contradict – focus on what the speaker is saying.* In this process, you'll need to manage a desire to interrupt, to correct or to use phrases like 'Yes, but…'

Rules for both

Your turn will come… and this means allowing the other person to complete their thought process and say what needs to be said, in short sections paraphrased by you as you listen. Then take your turn. You may find it helpful to nominate a facilitator to manage the conversation or use a physical object to indicate who 'has the floor'.

How to keep getting better

Remember that when people's ideas, contributions and suggestions are not actioned, or where there is disagreement, they may easily feel that they have not been 'listened to'. This underlines the importance of ensuring that others are properly heard and are part of the conversation.

To help you succeed with this technique in developing listening meetings, you will need to review your performance as a conversation group. Set aside three minutes at the end of meetings and check in on the following two questions:

1. What went well using this technique?
2. What do we need to focus on to improve our next conversation?

Listening in virtual meetings

The speaker/listener technique works well in online meetings, where individual contributions may often be difficult to manage. You might find it a good place to start the practice of structured listening conversations and, although remote, people will appreciate being given the space to express themselves fully. Remote conversations make it difficult to read the full picture in terms of how others are feeling – what's known as a 'low-context' environment. This means the full sensory picture on which we can rely when in the room with colleagues is no longer available to us and we can only make sense of the conversation based on what we see and hear. This is often a poorly lit image with an unhelpful camera angle and inadequate microphone, and there may well be background distractions too. Using the speaker/listener technique will allow each person to say what needs to be said and know that it has been heard and understood. It's an opportunity to add real connection to conversations that may otherwise be just transactional, incomplete or lead to misunderstanding.

How the technique helps conversations about inclusion

One of the most important and valuable contributions a leader can make to an organization is to face into conversations that need to be held about inclusion. These conversations go straight to the heart of what can be so difficult about listening. It is uncomfortable to anticipate what we might hear and concerning to anticipate how we might feel when we hear it. The speaker/listener technique won't soothe those fears, but using it will ensure that the people in your business who have a right to be heard and who have something they need to say will feel and be heard, and that is the gift of relying on a process such as this to maximize the impact you can have on changing working lives for the better.

The listeners:
The conflict-resolution expert

Ben Yeger is a conflict transformation expert, consultant, peace activist in the context of the Israeli Palestine conflict, and is a movement medicine teacher.[5] He has used his skills and experience to broker conversations between Israelis and Palestinians since 2007. As an ex-Israeli soldier, Ben's views on the challenge of questioning the way we are conditioned to label others in conflict conversations are fascinating. A combination of this personal odyssey and his skills as a therapist have given him powerful insights on listening.

What struck me in our conversation was the value Ben places on slowing down – he feels that speaking so people can actually hear you demonstrates that you really want to be heard, which in turn enables others to listen.

I was interested to hear Ben talk about the importance of being clear about what you can take as a listener – what bandwidth is available to you in a situation. In the search to find a solution, he cautions,

---

[5] www.movingconflicts.org.

there is a risk that we might be more ambitious than the other person is about finding it. This stops us from listening to what is actually happening as we seek to impose what we see as the way forward.

Ben has some excellent advice for listeners:

- Listen from the heart – with whatever you call love.
- Slow down inside yourself as you listen and respond.
- Acknowledge and learn the goodness of listening.

3

I've got shift to do
Managing your impact

Where we learn to listen to ourselves and how to listen to others.

- Learning to listen to yourself.
- Developing empathy.
- How to listen.
- Setting your intention.

Learning to listen to yourself

You're a busy person. I know that because of the research that tells us about organizational productivity, burnout and the 'always-on' culture in which we live. Whether you are working remotely, in the office or a blend of the two, it's likely that you are under pressure, with a lot of unfinished tasks nagging away at you.

Why does that matter to you as a listener? It matters because to be able to listen fully requires the discipline of parking distractions and being present for the conversation.

This might require a different approach, but it's hard to imagine anyone being able to listen effectively without learning how to become fully present.

So let's take a look at what you might need to do.

Four ways to listen to yourself

1. Create space

Therapy sessions of any nature tend to be booked by the hour, but last only 50 minutes. Those precious 10 minutes left to the therapist allow them the time to complete any notes, take a comfort break and, crucially, refocus themselves to prepare for their next session. This discipline serves both the therapist and the client, reducing 'rush' and allowing the practitioner to create an atmosphere conducive to listening.

2. Mindshift

When leaders address differences between leading and managing in training forums, it's fascinating to see them reflect on how addictive it is to get cracking on stuff that they can tick off a to-do list. A colleague of mine describes this as solving puzzles, not problems. Here's a typical example of how the list might break down.

Puzzles	Problems
Emails	Setting vision
Meetings	Exploring culture
Zoom	Organizational design
Creating templates	Understanding colleagues
Putting a presentation together	and customers
Performance reviews	Raising money to invest in the future
Operational stuff	
Finding a hot desk	
Solving technology issues	

Problems can be emotionally challenging – they can remain incomplete for a long time, take on a life of their own, continue to grow. But puzzles are satisfying evidence of output, completion, achievement. Under pressure, it's human nature to revert to puzzles, where we can feel certain and avoid problems – where uncertainty thrives. This often-adrenalized activity, fuelled by caffeine, no breaks and multitasking is the very opposite of what we need to be able to become present and listen well as the pull of finishing stuff draws us away from a deeper conversation. Have you ever tried to have a conversation with someone who is writing an email at the same time? It isn't the most satisfying exchange you'll ever have had – it will have been transactional at best. There is no space to engage in the conversation from the listener's perspective and the speaker's space is squeezed into micro-seconds of attention from the listener, in which it is necessary to articulate the problem, idea or solution that needs to be discussed.

Listening is an integral part of the problem side of the table. Your conversations will need to be listening conversations, but you won't be able to engage fully unless you take the route of creating space for yourself to settle, feel prepared and consider the atmosphere you need to create.

How long do you need to centre yourself and be ready to listen? Only you can know. The first step is to check in with yourself.

1. Am I solving puzzles or problems?
2. What is my equivalent of the 50-minute hour and how can I make it work for me?

Creating space in the workplace can be hard – but it can be just as hard working from home with the multitude of distractions that are likely to draw our attention.

Give yourself the best chance you can of listening to *yourself* by creating the space that works best for you. Take a few minutes now to consider the next point.

3. Work out when and where you do your best thinking

Have a think about when and where you do your best thinking… It might be:

- walking the dog
- running
- in the shower
- in the car
- in bed.

Perhaps these resonate with you – in any event, I've rarely – if ever – heard someone say, 'At my computer', or 'On MS Teams'. All of the responses I've listed are created by space – moments of regular, flowing movement or quiet, unpressured time when you can access deeper memories and when your brainwaves are slower. These are the moments when we can really listen to ourselves and notice how we are feeling. In these moments, you will be able to reflect on how you want to engage with others to solve some of the problems you face in your work. The solutions are there if you can just listen to your inner voice by creating space for it to be heard.

4. Noticing

It will be difficult for you to notice what's going on for others as you listen to them if you find it hard to notice what's going on for you. This is the principle of self-awareness highlighted by Daniel Goleman in his book *Emotional Intelligence*.[1]

---

[1] Daniel Goleman, *Emotional Intelligence*, 1995.

Goleman's model of emotional intelligence, also known as emotional quotient (EQ) has evolved over the years, but what seems to be a stable interpretation of it is the ability to monitor our own emotion and those of other people.

How are you feeling right now? Tired? Excited? Ponderous? A study published in 2017[2] identified 27 different types of emotion, so what you're experiencing right now may be a complex mix. In 1984, Professor Paul Ekman[3] found there were seven basic emotions, which he later revised down to six. There may be debate about the numbers, but one thing is certain: we all feel emotions, however we want to define them.

As a listener, you will benefit from noticing what emotions you are feeling so you can choose how to deal with them. They may also be emotions that arise as a result of how you feel about the person with whom you will be in conversation, or the effect a situation may be having on you. It's vital to notice.

In case you're feeling a wide range of emotional responses as you reflect on this challenge, here's the list of 27 for you to consider:

Admiration	Adoration	Aesthetic appreciation
Amusement	Anxiety	Awe
Awkwardness	Boredom	Calm
Confusion	Craving	Disgust
Empathetic pain	Entrancement	Envy

---

[2] Alan S. Cowen and Dacher Keltner, 'Self-report captures 27 distinct categories of emotion bridged by continuous gradients'. Available from www.pnas.org [accessed 21 March 2021].

[3] K. Scherer and P. Ekman, *Approaches to Emotion*, 1984.

Excitement	Fear	Horror
Interest	Joy	Nostalgia
Romance	Sadness	Satisfaction
Sexual desire	Sympathy	Triumph

Mindfulness

In recent years, mindfulness has gained significant traction as a noticing practice to include in daily life. Professor Mark Williams, former Director of the Oxford Mindfulness Centre, says that mindfulness means knowing directly what is going on inside and outside ourselves, moment by moment. This valuable practice has proved life-changing for many people, and research in the field continues to develop suggesting there may be benefits in motivation and productivity for those who practise it. Whatever you feel about mindfulness, or meditation of any kind, it's worth experimenting with a version of it to increase your ability to notice.

Check out the mindfulness practice in the listening resources at www.listeningshift.com if you'd like to test out how a mindfulness experience feels.

Another way to approach noticing is to consider our *mindlessness*. Reflecting on how automatically we respond in conversation, or how habitually we approach everyday situations, might help to redefine a methodology for noticing going forward.

Harvard Psychology Professor Ellen Langer[4] is renowned for her work on mindfulness without meditation – something she defines as the ordinary, everyday capacity each

---

[4] Ellen J. Langer, *Mindfulness*, 1991.

of us has to notice new things. She defines mindlessness as 'characterized by an entrapment in old categories; by automatic behaviour that precludes attending to new signals; and by action that operates from a single perspective'.

I love the way she demonstrates this concept by rewriting the story of Little Red Riding Hood:

> Once upon a time there was a mindless little girl named Little Red Riding Hood. One day, when she went to visit her ailing grandmother, she was greeted by a wolf dressed in her grandmother's nightclothes. 'What big eyes you have, Grandma,' she exclaimed, clueless as ever, although she had seen her grandmother's eyes countless times before.

Noticing is about avoiding the automatic – Little Red Riding Hood obviously sees her grandmother so often that she's stopped looking at her properly. As we know, this goes on to apply to Grandma's newly deepened voice and the size of her teeth. Little Red Riding Hood is doing what we all do – relying on 'automatic pilot', making assumptions about reliable truths. She is so certain she is in front of her grandmother that she thinks she doesn't need to be fully, mindfully present. Certainty is her downfall.

Langer describes certainty as 'a cruel mindset'. She suggests that certainty 'hardens our minds against possibility and closes them to the world we actually live in'.

There is a place for certainty in leadership, of course. Earlier, when we considered how you might listen more deeply across your organization, I mentioned the importance of certainty in providing clarity – in following up as and when we have promised to do so. That's important for building confidence and trust, but here we are applying the principle of noticing. Might it be that experiencing a powerful sense of certainty in some of your conversations could be a useful indicator that you are not listening enough?

Before certainty becomes a modus operandi, keep your mind open by listening to yourself and others to keep curiosity, flexibility and agility at the heart of your decision-making. Don't get eaten by the Big Bad Wolf.

Everyday practices to improve noticing

1. How am I feeling?

On a scale of 1–10, where 1 is low and 10 is the best you've ever felt, give yourself an instinctive number to reflect how you are feeling in this very moment. Then unpick the reasons for being at that number.

Consider the number from different perspectives – what's contributing to the overall score? Is it a physical assessment? Emotional? Or what's on your mind – your thoughts? For example, '4 out of 10 today. I've been sitting down for too long, feeling stressed. Thinking about the conversation I had this morning and can't stop replaying it in my mind.'

As a facilitator, I would also call this exercise 'Clearing Listening'. It's a system of noticing what might get in the way of me being fully present – listing all the things that are taking up space in my head... and therefore blocking my ability to notice anything else. In Gestalt psychology, this is known as unfinished business. Whatever you choose to call it, practising it daily, or twice daily – or more – will allow you to develop a shortcut to preparing yourself to be fully present and available to listen well.

This exercise also works well with a word choice. Limit yourself to one word that sums up how you feel in the moment – be as instinctive as you can in choosing the word quickly. Then unpick why that word sprang to mind in the same way, using physical, emotional and mental insight.

2. Breathing

Paying attention to how you breathe will reap so many benefits, many of which are well documented and known about. I'm particularly interested in the infectious nature of breathing. As a performer, I'm well aware that if I'm nervous, holding my breath high in my body and gulping in short breaths, my audience will start to 'sigh out', trying to breathe on my behalf. I'll see them fidgeting, uncomfortable and probably not aware of why they are responding in that way. I have witnessed people in conversations holding their breath as they wait for the other person to finish talking… raising stress levels for both parties and definitely not conducive to listening. And we are all aware of that wonderful sigh – the breathing out that we might experience as we arrive somewhere lovely to rest and recuperate. Home on a Friday night, a weekend away, a holiday in the sun. Breathing controls our emotional state, which influences our behaviour, and this is what influences those around us. It's worth managing this as a listener because how you breathe may be subconsciously influencing the conversation and this can work both for you and against you.

Try the following breathing exercises to manage your state, gain control and increase your presence. For breathing exercises, you may find it helpful to be on your own, sitting well, eyes closed. But the exercises below can be done anywhere, as long as you can discipline yourself to focus in on the breath effectively. Once mastered, they're an easy route to preparing yourself to engage in any conversation in a calm, neutral state.

- *Box breathing:* Breathe in for a count of 4, hold your breath for a count of 4, breathe out for a count of 4, wait for a count of 4. Repeat.
- *4, 7, 8 breath:* Breathe in for a count of 4, hold your breath for a count of 7, breathe out for a count of 8. Repeat four times.
- *Temperature breath:* Breathe in and out through your nose for this one – easy, normal breathing, no extra effort required. As you breathe in, the air will feel cool as it enters your nostrils and warmer as you breathe out. It's a simple noticing exercise, but great for practice.

3. Noticing your surroundings – auditory

This is a lovely way to extend noticing if you've got a couple of minutes. Sit or stand – as long as you're comfortable. Take a minute to adjust to the environment by being still and quiet. Then shift your attention to what you can hear in your immediate surroundings. Maybe nothing, maybe some familiar everyday sounds of technology working. Just notice. Then shift your attention a little further away – outside the room that you're in. Then further to outside the home or building you're in. Try to detect the furthest away sound you can possibly hear and all the sounds in between back to where you are at this precise moment.

It's a great way to become present – to become fully aware of your surroundings and be in the moment.

4. Noticing your surroundings – visual

Finally, have a look at the space you're in. Notice what you can about the environment and what's in it – how it's all laid out. Then look away or close your eyes momentarily. You're going to repeat this three times.

- Look at the space you're in again as if you are a child – maybe six or seven years old. What are the opportunities for fun and destruction in this space?
- Look at the space as if you are responsible for cleaning it – what's going to cause you effort, what's easy to break?
- Finally, look at the space as if you were a designer – what are the possibilities for changing it? What would cause you difficulties in your redesign and where's the potential for improvement?

As you think about improving your listening, you might take this exercise a stage further. If you have a big conversation with a colleague or customer, how might the environment either support or challenge the conversation's outcome?[5] How does the space look to the other person as they arrive?

---

[5] Leslie S. Greenberg and Wanda Malcolm, 'Resolving unfinished business: Relating process to outcome', *Journal of Counselling and Clinical Psychology*, 70(2), 406–416 (2002).

I've heard many leaders say that their door is always open… but how will people feel when they walk in? Only noticing will give you the answer.

Watch your thoughts, they become your words; watch your words, they become your actions; watch your actions, they become your habits; watch your habits, they become your character; watch your character, it becomes your destiny.

Lao Tsu

The listeners:
The mindfulness coach

Damion Wonfor is an executive coach, facilitator, coach supervisor and mindfulness teacher. His view is that practising mindfulness is integral to being an effective listener and he credits his own practice with helping him to be present – personally and professionally – while navigating life's challenges.

As a listener, Damion says mindfulness offers two keys:

1. We find the ability to keep our mind where we want it to be.
2. We become aware of how we are relating to what we're experiencing.

He recommends checking in with yourself by asking the following questions as often as you can to enhance your noticing... and transform your listening:

1. What's going on for me?
2. What am I experiencing and how am I relating to it?

In our conversation, we agreed that this is essential practice as a listener facing big or challenging conversations where we are likely to feel defensive – conflict situations, addressing diversity, embracing inclusion, understanding the impact of change in a team or organization. Noticing what's going on for you may involve other intelligences – a physical reaction, an emotional one or something involving your intuition. He advocates using all that's available to you and not just focusing on what you're thinking.

I interpret Damion's approach using this example: When challenged in an argument, I may:

- Think: 'They're wrong and I'm going to prove them wrong.'
- Feel: My throat tighten, my face flush and my fists clench.
- Sense/intuit: There's something else going on here that hasn't been addressed.

Having mindfully listened to this range of intelligences, and by being fully present, I can make a choice about how to respond. Damion describes this as paying attention to early warning signals and says it develops our ability to trust ourselves as listeners.

His advice is:

1. Take a breath – we are mostly on auto-pilot when we listen, which allows our mind to wander.

2. Feel your feet, feel your seat – notice points of contact as a way of bringing yourself into the moment.

3. Be curious – when we get interested, we pay attention.

Why empathy is helpful

You won't be surprised to hear that empathy tends to make us better listeners. But there are different sorts of empathy for us to consider – personal, social, emotional and cognitive – and this section will explore when and how each can affect our listening.

Empathy is essential as a leader – understanding what life is like for people working across the business is key to building communities where people thrive and are able to – and want to – do their best work. Some people are more naturally empathetic than others, but it seems to be a muscle that we can flex. It is possible to work at empathy and become skilled at it. What is unarguable is that if we are to develop empathy, or demonstrate it, we will need to listen. How can we achieve understanding if we haven't fully listened to the landscape described to us?

Curiosity is key…

Social empathy

To listen fully in conversations which are essential to the diversity and inclusion agenda in your organization, you'll need to explore and develop your social empathy.

We are more familiar with the idea of empathizing with someone in a particular experience, a conversation that often allows us in some way to recognize the situation being described to us. These 'I know what you mean' conversations cover a huge range from frustrations about commuting to the sad loss of a loved one, and anything in between. Empathizing in these conversations may feel hard, but the shared insights from these common experiences mean we can more easily connect.

Social empathy requires us to understand what life is or has been like for a community where 'I know what you mean' is much less likely to have meaning. These are conversations with groups whose lives and experiences are not shared by us. We may have absolutely no idea what they have experienced, and this is where the harder work of listening kicks in as we try to understand, without having any personal insight on which we can rely to show an understanding of the wider context.

In society, this might be broadening our perspective about the lives of black people, indigenous people and people of colour, or the lesbian, gay, bisexual, transgender and queer (LGBTQ) community, or perhaps developing a greater understanding of people who have experienced food poverty.

In your organization, it might be about groups of people who work on the frontline of your business, in operations, in factories and in branches, or understanding people who have felt marginalized, silenced or ignored. You may not have any direct connection to, or experience of, any of this.

The challenge here is to probe the conversation not to understand how we might cope if we had been through the experiences shared ourselves, but to reach a place of understanding where we realize what it has been like from the perspective of the other person.

In other words, you may hear from a person who has been repeatedly overlooked for promotion, had their opinions and ideas rejected in meetings only to see or hear them enacted by someone else, or not been able to join teambuilding events because they were not inclusive. Hearing stories like this, you might empathize by imagining how you would feel... but that isn't enough. You need to really listen to get into the shoes of the other person and start walking.

In 2015 *The New York Times* published an article damning the workplace conditions at Amazon.[6] Highly critical of management practices and using anecdotes from employees, the article shook the business, which was strongly defended by some of the leadership and critical of the journalism. Jeff Bezos himself responded by saying, 'The article doesn't describe the Amazon I know or the caring Amazonians I work with every day.'

I have no idea what it's like to work at Amazon, but I think Jeff Bezos's defence is interesting. Perhaps if he regularly worked in the warehouses and talked to the people there, he might find a different Amazonian perspective. The Amazon he knows, and the Amazonians with whom he works every day, will not give him a complete perspective of the lives of everyone working in the Amazonian community. Perhaps he does do this, but the defensive nature of his response seeks to close the conversation down – his response does not suggest a willingness to listen.

Between 1997 and 2002, the BBC produced five series of 'Back to the Floor'. These programmes allowed a CEO

---

[6] Jodi Kantor and David Streitfeld, 'Inside Amazon: Wrestling big ideas in a bruising workplace', in *New York Times*, 15 August 2015.

or senior executive to go undercover to discover what the life of a new-starter or entry level role was like in the businesses the leader ran from the boardroom. It was captivating TV and they gained priceless perspective from truth-telling employees who had no idea, until the big reveal at the end of the show, that they were sharing confidences with the most powerful people in the business. It was empathy in action as the undercover leader listened to the stories of how the business treated its people and always prompted deep reflections and some tough conversations back at company HQ. The leader would then trigger significant action intended to improve the lives, motivations and support of people in the business.

Whilst you may not want to wear a disguise to open a dialogue with your employees, you may benefit yourself and them by opening up conversations that encourage an honest appraisal of what life is like for the communities in your company. To be effective, these conversations will have to go beyond polite or managed messages. How will you demonstrate a commitment to listening – to hearing the truths that give you real perspective into your colleagues' lives?

Developing empathy

For actors, an ability to empathize with a character's experience allows them to recreate emotions that will affect audiences. Drawing on connections from their own experience allows for powerful – and authentic – emotion played in the scene or drama.

A way to flex your empathy muscle is to do the same. Draw on your own experiences to find out how another person may be feeling – their experience may not be the same or directly connected, but you can use those emotions and senses you felt to connect to others.

Footballer Marcus Rashford used his own childhood experience of sometimes going hungry to fire his energy in campaigning for free meals for children who need them during school holidays.

Rashford's hard-working single mother sometimes struggled to put food on the table for her family, and his respect for her efforts – and those of other parents in similar situations – shows that he has listened to and understood the challenges faced by those in food poverty. His empathy for their situation, and those of their children, has affected millions of people who offered practical and financial support and got behind the campaign for the government to change its position of not offering meal support during half-term holidays. His exemplary calm, tenacious approach touches us – we can see how he feels it. We trust him because he understands.

Jacinda Ardern, elected New Zealand's Prime Minister in 2017, is also celebrated for her empathy and understanding. Unafraid to show human emotion in the face of tragedy and determined to include voices from all parts of the Māori culture represented in her cabinet, she represents a distinctly different leadership proposition and is proud to be driven by her curiosity to understand the lives, communities and cultures of the citizens she leads. In her case, she is able to empathize not because she has directly relatable experience, but because she has made it her job to find out.

I'm proudly focused on empathy, because you can be both empathetic and strong.
New Zealand Prime Minister Jacinda Ardern

Affective memory exercise

Used in method actor training, this process helps to find a connection between one person's experiences and those of another. The connection is the emotions felt – the actual experience does not have to be related or the same. It is an accessible way of creating empathy by using sensory recall to revisit the experience. You can take a light touch with this or think very deeply, depending on the situation.

> Joe has acquired a small marketing business employing 30 staff. He will be retaining 15 of the staff from the business and letting the others go. Those being retained will need to be integrated into Joe's existing team of 35 people who are well-established, socially involved, long-time employees. Both sets of employees are feeling worried about their change in circumstances. The concerns of Joe's current employees are focused on how the culture of the business will change and how much the success of the integration depends on their inclusivity skills. The incoming employees are upset about their colleagues' redundancies and unsure about how life will be working under new leadership, in a new office environment with a new team.
>
> How can Joe empathize fully with those involved and work towards supporting both sides to become a cohesive group who work well together in growing the business and validating the investment?

Harnessing empathy

Joe recalls a childhood experience of leaving one town and moving to another, involving a change of school. He left a close group of friends behind and knew no one in his new school. This affective memory will help him recall how he felt, so he can connect with people in his business during this time of change.

Step 1: What emotions were felt?

In Joe's case, he remembers feeling resentful – forced to leave his friends by his parents' choices.

He also recalls feeling anxious – sick with nerves about walking through the school gates on the first day of term.

He also felt lonely, although only briefly at the start of the day.

Step 2: Sense memory

- *Sight:* Joe recalls everything he can remember seeing on his first day at the new school... buildings, faces, colours, shapes, sizes. Anything and everything he can recall associated with what he saw that day.
- *Sound:* Joe recalls what he heard – the radio station playing at home, the sounds of the family having breakfast before leaving for school, the playground noise before the bell rings to start school.

- *Smell:* Joe recalls the smell of coffee brewing at home, of burnt toast; he remembers the bleached smell of the school corridors, wafts of scent worn by a member of staff in his first class.
- *Taste:* Joe recalls his nerves, which made his breakfast toast taste like cardboard; he could taste a metallic anxiety in his mouth all morning until lunchtime when things were improving, and he enjoyed a cheese sandwich and apple.
- *Touch:* Joe recalls giving his father a hug and not wanting to let go before leaving the house. Distracted, he jammed his finger in his locker and remembers it stinging and then aching all day. He remembers sitting in his classroom on a hard chair. He remembers how smoothly the keys on the keyboard in the computer room typed.

Using your senses to connect to a memory allows for a powerful recall of an event that can otherwise easily be glossed over. It's a route to empathy for Joe with his new team – remembering how new and unfamiliar things were and how isolating the experience was of his first morning.

This is a brief example, but Joe could go into a lot of detail, allowing his thoughts to drift back and exploring the day again.

Having done this exercise, Joe can listen to the concerns of those involved who want to speak up. Remembering his own emotional reaction in this situation takes the fear of hearing others' emotions away. He knows it's an unsettling time, can identify with people's feelings and will be able to demonstrate empathy as he listens.

Empathy questions

Take time to reflect on the following questions as part of your planning process towards understanding the mindset, behaviours and actions of the person or people with whom you need to build connections:

1. What's the other person's *perception* of the situation?
2. What might be *troubling* them about it?
3. What *emotions* might they be *feeling*?
4. What might they *need*?

Joe might use these questions to reflect on the motivations and behaviours of the people involved in his company integration.

Possible perceptions of existing employees

This is a merger that has been imposed on them. They're expected to work differently to integrate the new team. Management is more focused on profit than employee happiness. The new workload is going to create stress.

What might be troubling them

Am I going to be replaced? What if the new team outperforms our existing one? Everything will change – it won't be the same place to work. As the business grows, more and more work is going to be pushed my way.

Emotions they may be feeling

Resentment, anxiety, hostility, being overwhelmed, apathy.

What they might need

Reassurance, clarity, regular communication, team-building, a steady pace. Don't try to do too much at once – be patient.

Taking it further: Empathy mapping

In design, creators are often asked to build an empathy map, allowing the customers' reaction to or use of the product or service to guide the design process.

We can take these principles and translate them into an empathy strategy that allows us to consider the context and perspective of the people we need to listen to – and to influence.

The questions to consider are:

- What are people seeing?
- What are they hearing?
- What motivates them?
- What scares them?
- What do they think and feel?
- What do they say?

See whether you can use these questions to reflect on a key person in your life with whom you would like to build a better relationship. What new perspective does it offer you?

Which type of empathy seems right for the context?

You may have a view about how naturally empathetic you feel yourself to be. Empathy has a number of definitions – it's a broad and complex area. What matters in relation to listening is to consider the following:

1. *Emotional empathy.* This is how we find ourselves affected by the emotions we witness someone experiencing – for example, crying because someone else is crying or feeling disgusted because someone is describing a disgusting experience. This propensity to feel what another person is feeling appears powerful but it's not ideal for listening, as we can easily be

swept up in the emotion of the situation and then it becomes about us – we are seizing the experience and personalizing it.

2. *Cognitive empathy.* This is a rational recognition of what someone is describing. It is feeling, but with a cool head.

Both types of empathy demonstrate understanding, but for your leadership listening, the more objective analysis may allow you to listen in the moment and focus your attention on the other person rather than indulge in the emotions that move you.

Can you have too much empathy?

There is no doubt that empathy can get in the way of a rational approach to decision-making. In his book *The Wisdom of Psychopaths,*[7] Kevin Dutton says that some professions benefit from psychopathic traits – people who are only minimally empathetic may be able to make life-changing decisions on behalf of others by thinking in a logical, level-headed, calm way. Imagine an anxious pilot paralysed by emotion and unable to make a crisis-averting decision because they are so worried about what might happen to all the passengers if they get it wrong? In that situation, we might all want somebody who isn't too empathetic.

I notice that some of my clients who are highly empathetic worry far more than others about the impact they are making in their role. They may find themselves nervous and agitated before a press conference or presentation; they may

---

[7] Kevin Dutton, *The Wisdom of Psychopaths*, 2013.

feel anxious about a feedback conversation or delivering bad news; they may feel uncomfortable about delivering a board update or challenging colleagues to do more. Concerns about how their messages will be received can hold them back from achieving their full potential – they are sometimes constrained by empathy and not helped by it.

Commercial decisions may also be harder if you are a highly empathetic person. Having to reduce staff numbers in a business where colleagues have been long-serving and loyal may make the decision hard. You may find yourself reflecting on how the news will impact their family life, think about how that person might manage financially, worry how easily they will find another role on the level at which they've been operating. It can be a long list. For some, this might delay those tough decisions, causing the business harm. For others, the cost is personal – stress, affected sleep, change in appetite. It makes being less empathetic sound appealing.

However, it is important not to let this recognition that you can overdo empathy put you off developing it. Most of us need to work much harder at being in the shoes of others.

Deciding that too much empathy may have a negative affect is an excuse to step away from deep listening. Stay curious…

The listeners: The Samaritan

Maggie Cameron MBE has been a Samaritan for 11 years. In her view, listening is the foundation of understanding... as she says, 'How can you know what's going on if you don't listen?'

In our conversation, I asked Maggie about suspending judgement as a listener and I was struck by her response. She reminded me that as soon as we've decided what's going on, we stop listening. Since many of us are driven to fix, to solve problems, the search to find and offer a solution can be a powerful motivator... but as soon as we believe we have the answer to the other person's problem, we base everything else on that idea. We stop listening.

To manage this, she recommends that we try to stop worrying about what we are going to say next. The ability to do this well develops as we become more comfortable with silence... allowing time to process what we've heard.

Maggie sees the role of a listener as a sounding board – and advocates for reflecting back what you hear as a transformative tool. It's a simple strategy. If you're not sure what to say, she says, reflect back what the other person has just said. You often find that they agree as if they've heard it for the first time – and perhaps they have.

Even though Samaritans hear painful and difficult stories of the lives of others, Maggie finds this is a way of helping her appreciate what she has in her own life. She says, 'You learn so much more if you let others talk.'

She has some wise advice for improving your listening:

- Give people time – time and space to talk are essential to help people process what's going on for them.
- Silence any distractions – turn off your phone and computer. You can't listen if anything is going to get in your way.
- Be present – don't see yourself as there to influence or guide the other person. Just be there as a sounding board.

How to listen

'What you say is your stuff, what I hear is my stuff.'

We understand our own reasons for taking action, behaving in a certain way, holding the beliefs we do. This self-serving bias is hard-wired into our psyche so that from our own perspective, our decisions and behaviours are clear, rational and reasonable. We can spend a good deal of thinking and reflection time reviewing those same actions and repeatedly making sense of them so that anyone who doesn't understand or respond with the same insight is bewildering. How could they not get something that is so obvious?

We don't tend to afford others the same depth of understanding – in fact, we may take their behaviours and actions at face value and start to label them accordingly. Do you know anyone who 'always' behaves the same way? 'Never' changes their approach? The longer we know someone, the more likely we are to feel able to anticipate their actions, to 'know' what they're thinking or how they will respond to a situation. Behavioural scientists refer to this as closeness-communication bias, which is particularly relevant in romantic relationships, but also applies to anyone we spend enough time with to feel we could anticipate their responses.

You might argue that this insight built over time is a great shortcut in decision-making. It's a sign that your invested efforts in connecting with that person are paying off, that you will be 'on the same page', 'have each other's backs' and can have deeper conversations that develop the relationship further. All of this may be true, but if we feel we already know how a person will respond, then what's the point of asking the question? All too often, it seems that we don't ask and if we ask at all, we don't listen to the response because we've already processed what we assume it will be.

About 15 years ago, I ran a series of coaching sessions with the managing director of a bank. He would always ask me how I was, and I would always respond positively – as I do 99.9% of the time to anyone who asks after my wellbeing. But on this particular day, I was feeling pretty terrible. There was a lot going on for me at home, and I was stressed and under pressure. We met in the reception area of the bank and he asked, as usual, how I was. I can't remember the exact words I used in response, but I had decided to be frank with him because by now we knew each other relatively well and I thought I could trust him with an honest answer, so I said, 'Not great, actually...' and was about to explain when he breezily replied with 'Good, good. Glad to hear it!' I should say that he is a really nice person, a good leader, a family man. He was mortified when I eventually drew attention to his lack of listening (I didn't do it at that time, but later in the session when he was in a better listening mode).

I'm conscious that I often reply to the question 'How are you?' with a standard 'Fine, thanks', because I can tell that the person asking the question is not really available to listen to the answer. It's a habit, a social convention, a way of getting into the meat of a conversation that would be weird without this fleeting, cursory 'hello'.

If we start a conversation by paying so little attention, it's going to be difficult to turn up the dial as we continue the discussion. Start as you mean to go on.

A practice opportunity

Before we take a deeper look at how to listen well, let's start with the greeting, 'How are you?'

Spend a day deliberately asking people this introductory question, as you might anyway… and use this checklist as a way of noticing your usual approach and taking it to the next level as a listener.

1. Check in with yourself… are you ready to pay attention? To notice? To listen?
2. Decide to be present.
3. Ask the question.
4. Notice what they say in response, and how they say it – pay close attention to the full context of words, voice tone, body language, facial expression, energy.
5. If you get a standard reply – 'Fine, thanks' – probe a little deeper… see whether you can uncover what 'fine' really means to them. Try asking something like 'What's fine on a scale of 1 to 10?'
6. Offer an observation – 'I noticed a spring in your step this morning!' or 'You're walking a little slower than usual today… deep in thought?'

These small observations are an indication of your desire to notice the other person. Being seen may be as vital as being heard. In the briefest of exchanges, you are showing that you are available to listen and that you have every intention of being ready to do so.

Alison Wood Brooks,[8] an associate professor at Harvard Business School, describes this progression in a casual greeting as using 'follow-up questions'. She describes these follow-up questions as having 'special powers'. Using follow-up questions allows people to become fully engaged and feel valued. Who wouldn't want that in their business?

Notice how setting the tone feels for you and consider how you might apply it more broadly. What percentage of the time do you feel you could commit to this type of follow-up when greeting others?

Why we listen

Sociologist Charles Derber[9] found in his research that in conversation we might be looking to support the other person in our responses – or, more likely, to find a way of bringing the conversation back to ourselves. Derber calls this 'conversational narcissism', and his thesis details how modern conversation is becoming increasingly self-interested.

You might recognize the conversation starter examples below, either because you have used the tactic yourself, or you'll have experienced it in talking with others.

---

[8] Alison Wood Brooks and Leslie K. John, 'The surprising power of questions', in *Harvard Business Review*, May–June 2018. Available from https://hbr.org/2018/05/the-surprising-power-of-questions [accessed 9 February 2021].
[9] Charles Derber, *The Pursuit of Attention: Power and Ego in Everyday Life*, 2000.

Listening to support

> *Colleague:* I've got so much on at work right now. Not sure how I'm going to cope.
> *Manager:* That sounds tough. What's the biggest challenge?

This type of conversational response is especially helpful if you are coaching others at work or supporting their development in some way. It's vital that we master the art of support in conversation – particularly as we learn more about having conversations around issues relating to mental health and transforming commitments to diversity and inclusion.

The focus is on creating the space for the other person to investigate and express how they are feeling. You're focusing the conversation on them – not on yourself.

Listening to switch back to ourselves

> *Colleague:* I've got so much on at work right now. Not sure how I'm going to cope.
> *Manager:* Ugh – I know. You should see what's just landed on my desk this morning.

The manager is much more interested in using the colleague's statement to share their own personal stress. Without acknowledging what has been said at all, the manager pulls the conversation straight back to them. But this response is not always negative. It can be valuable to help create empathy in a conversation, as long as your attention – and intention – is based on bringing the conversation back to the person who expressed the issue in the first place. For example, the manager might go on to say:

Colleague: I've got so much on at work right now. Not sure how I'm going to cope.

Manager: Ugh – I know. You should see what's just landed on my desk this morning. Would it help to talk things through?

This might lead to a conversation that helps both of them – as long as balance is observed and they listen well to each other, this may be exactly what they both need to manage their respective situations. Unfortunately, this seems a less likely outcome than our manager staying with their own agenda and then heading off to start their day.

This is a simple way of reviewing how we conduct ourselves in conversations generally, or in particular interactions. We will all have deployed this switching response with others, even if it was well intended.

Listening to solve

Colleague: I've got so much on at work right now. Not sure how I'm going to cope.

Manager: Right. Well first of all you need to get on top of the main account and then you should meet with the team on Slack this afternoon and let them know what you're not going to be able to deal with before it all gets out of hand.

As a leader, you may feel it is your responsibility to create the conditions for success in your team or organization. Your intention may be to support... but, in the case of this colleague and manager, the manager's response of solving the problem removes all autonomy from the colleague. This may increase their stress as they might feel that the manager thinks they're not capable of doing the job and could consequently feel threatened.

Over the long term, if the colleague continues to experience high levels of stress, they may find it becomes increasingly difficult to listen at all. The Karolynska Institute in Sweden[10] found a correlation between high levels of stress-induced cortisol and hearing problems such as tinnitus. Although this outcome might seem extreme, it is certainly easy to be distracted when we feel stressed. Competing thoughts and any physical reactions we may experience as our systems fight the feeling of threat won't help our listening.

Not being listened to well, or not feeling that you have been heard, can be stressful. It triggers frustration and feelings of being undermined and rejected, among other emotions. This is the risk of deploying the superficial principles of pretending to listen by nodding, making sounds of agreement and matching body language without the essential elements of being curious, demonstrating empathy and building genuine rapport. We usually know if it's not sincerely meant – we can sniff out the fakery. It makes things worse, not better.

We must all play our part in managing this by practising a better way of listening – by committing to improving our

---

[10] Dan Hasson et al., 'Stress and prevalence of hearing problems in the Swedish working population', in *BMC Public Health*, 130 (2011). Available from https://bmcpublichealth.biomedcentral.com/articles/10.1186/1471-2458-11-130 [accessed 9 February 2021].

support response in preference to switching the conversation back to our own pressing issues or solving those of others.

Nonetheless, context matters in our conversations and you will know what contribution context plays in your meetings, one-to-one discussions and personal relationships.

If two people in conversation are competing to listen, it's not going to be much of a conversation! But that, as my mother would say, would be a high-class problem. It just doesn't tend to happen. Most of the time, whatever our contribution, we are seeking to be heard and acknowledged, leading to a 'now you, now me' exchange as we make our point, wait while the other person speaks, then bring the topic back to ourselves.

Take a moment to reflect on your instinctive response in listening, but consider the context in which these states might apply. You may have a general sense of how you listen but see whether that changes with different groups or individuals. Are you the same with everyone or does it depend? What makes the difference?

It might help you to categorize your relationships as you reflect:

1. *Casual interactions*. These interactions might be occasional conversations with people with whom you have very little need to develop a personal or professional relationship. They might be transactional encounters in shops as you buy something or tradespeople who come to your home or business to help you. It may also be people you meet socially as a one-off experience at a specific event, or colleagues at work who you know, but don't work with as a rule.

2. *Your team or work colleagues.* These are frequent conversations with people with whom you collaborate, influence and engage. They will be important to you, but you may not know much about their personal lives, focusing on daily transactions and tasks to get the job done rather than more intimate or personal conversations.

3. *Social relationships.* These are friends, neighbours – people you have longer and deeper connections with. You may or may not see them often, but they are valued by you and are people whose company you would choose.

4. *Your inner circle.* These are your most immediate relationships with a partner, close friends and/or family with whom you live. They are the people you interact with most frequently and are your most important relationships.

When you've reflected on how you think you listen to these different groups, ask a couple of trusted colleagues, friends or family members what they experience in you as a listener. This is going to take courage – from you, and from them. It may be tough for them to be straight with you. However, their responses may lead to a great conversation. All you have to do is listen!

What's your approach to listening?

Score yourself using both the words and numbers. Don't overthink it – your instinctive assessment will ensure you avoid any justification that may excuse you from taking action.

Listening to support

Never		Rarely		Sometimes			Often		Always
1	2	3	4	5	6	7	8	9	10

Listening to switch the conversation back to you

Never		Rarely		Sometimes			Often		Always
1	2	3	4	5	6	7	8	9	10

Listening to solve

Never		Rarely		Sometimes			Often		Always
1	2	3	4	5	6	7	8	9	10

Note: You might assess yourself using 'sometimes' or applying a score between 5 and 7. This is okay – the reflection is still valuable. Is 'sometimes' good enough for you?

10 steps to listening well

In an ideal environment, we would all be able to inquire effortlessly in conversations – open-minded and accepting of each other with a sincere intention to fully understand and own our part in difficulties that arise. But, as with all things in life, there are days when events go well for us and days when, no matter how hard we try, nothing seems to quite line up. The same is true for communication – sometimes it's fluent, clear and flows, but at other times, we stumble and can't find the essence of what it is we are trying to get across to others.

As listeners, there will be days when the rapport doesn't click in, we misunderstand the other person or we desperately want to close the conversation down because the solution seems so obvious. I'll repeat... the process might be simple, but it's by no means easy.

I don't want to hold up the following 10 steps as a mechanical route to listening well so that each conversation becomes a checklist of points that we can tick and say 'I did that! I listened brilliantly.' That would never happen – and, of course, the best conversations come from a magic, a well-held space in which the words flow in the spirit of mutual respect. I sincerely hope you have more and more of those conversations.

On days when the going feels uphill, though, the steps here may be your friend. If something isn't working, have a think about where you missed an opportunity or what you found hardest. They'll help get the wheels in motion and carry you through when, and whether, you are finding listening hard.

For many years, I have been a devotee of hot yoga. I hate it. It's uncomfortable, mentally and physically challenging and time-consuming. I do it because I feel great afterwards and I believe in the health benefits it offers in combination with other exercise. One of the first teachers I had would urge the class on by saying repeatedly, 'If you can, you must...' I resented her whenever she said it, but I still responded. It made me aware that I could go further, do more, challenge myself to see what was possible in my practice. Without that nudge, I may get away with doing what I usually did and no more. I think of her often – and the words come back to me over and over again. I find them impossible to ignore, so now I pass them on to you as you start to listen well.

'If you can, you must...'

Step 1: Manage the judge

It is human nature to judge other people – an evolutionary instinct to work out whether the other person is someone we can trust or someone who is capable of making a successful contribution. In other words, we are judging their warmth and their competence on a scale known as the Stereotype Content Model (Fiske et al. 2002).[11] However, working out where the other person sits in terms of this scale may lead us to making assessments that prevent listening well.

As a listener for Samaritans in the United Kingdom, this principle of not judging others in order to listen well was something I had to work hard at mastering during my training. It turns out I form opinions fast and they can set my attitude for the duration of a conversation. I have found that to be something I have in common with many other people, and I don't take much pleasure in recognizing it.

Samaritans have conversations with many people who, for whatever reason, have taken paths in life that can be very difficult to hear about. But the listening volunteer role is to show empathy as we listen. No matter what we hear, it is hard to find empathy if we have already decided that the caller is in some way unworthy of our understanding because we disapprove of their choices in life. It's not for us to judge.

In organizations, where time and opportunity to talk may be limited because of the sheer number of tasks that

---

[11] Susan Fiske, Amy Cuddy, Peter Glick and Jun Xu, 'A model of (often mixed) stereotype content: Competence and warmth respectively follow from perceived status and competition', in *Journal of Personality and Social Psychology*, 82(6), 878–902 (2002).

need to be completed, judging may seem a shortcut to getting things done.

Some colleagues appear difficult and, as we've seen, it's easy to anticipate how others will respond if we know them very well. We may describe some customers as demanding, believe that some senior stakeholders 'don't get it', and view some team members as being 'not up to the job'.

Because we process what we think we've heard at approximately four times the speed at which we speak, there's always time to form a view or opinion – to make a judgement – about the other person.

If you're going to commit to improving your listening – to be known by the people in your business for being a present, attentive and supportive listening leader – you're going to have to let go of a judging mindset. Notice how you are feeling and what's going on for you, then take responsibility for it. This will free you up to practise step 2 with dedication.

Step 2: Be curious, not certain

Some of you will be inquisitive by nature and read this thinking, 'No problem – I can tick that off the list straight away.' Others will know that being curious depends on how interesting the other person is, the subject matter you are discussing or other factors – the situation, how much time you have, whether the subject is relevant to you.

But this step is non-negotiable. It is a must-do, a muscle to flex, a committed, minute-by-minute promise to become an inquirer. And it's not an 'eat your greens' obligation. Developing a mindset of curiosity will help you listen with ease – you'll be interested by what you hear, more and more questions will pop into your mind and the conversation will flow.

About 10 years ago, I was invited to work with a group of leaders from a mining organization. They were intelligent, fascinating people and I loved the opportunity to help them with their communication while finding out more about an industry with which I was unfamiliar. They were an international team and one of them had worked extensively in the Middle East. He was used to working in a hierarchical environment and was comfortable directing teams and using his immense presence as an influencing tool to establish authority. He listened to solve.

As I started to tap away at this ingrained approach, I set him a challenge. I told him I was about to recount a story about making a decision – presenting a personal dilemma I had experienced about two years previously for him to listen to. As he listened, I asked him to work out what my decision had been, based on how he heard me present the dilemma. I completed the story and then said to him, 'What decision do you think I made?' He looked at me, stood up to his full height (which was considerable) and said, 'What you should do is…' and proceeded to direct me as to how I should solve my issue.

I tell you this not to be critical of him – he was a man of many gifts – but he had learned that his role in life was to solve problems and direct other people to sort things out in doing so. He found it incredibly hard to listen any other way.

His painstaking practice was to develop a mindset of curiosity over certainty. Learning to have conversations with colleagues that invited depth of discussion and the exploration of a broad range of views was a challenge for him, but it was essential for his success in a culture so different from the one to which he had become accustomed.

Colombia University in the United States has been working with the concept of curiosity in conflict for some years now. Started by social psychologist Peter Coleman,[12] the Difficult Conversations Laboratory has studied the responses of huge numbers of people experiencing conflict. Part of the process is to encourage deeper exploration of the other person's point of view. Coleman suggests that if a dispute is presented to both parties as complex and multilayered, the conversation will be richer and ultimately more successful – even if those involved never agree, there is far greater understanding than in a dispute where a simple, binary argument is presented.[13]

The distinction is curiosity. If we can ask questions to build a more detailed picture, to develop our understanding of the complexity of the situation, to investigate the range of emotions a person may be experiencing, not only will we have listened well, but they will feel heard and understood. It is the holy grail of effective communication… but we're not quite there yet.

Step 3: Ask interested questions

I want to reframe the familiar phrase 'open questions' for two reasons: first, because we have become so used to hearing the expression that its meaning is reduced; and second,

---

[12] Katharina G. Kugler and Peter T. Coleman, 'Get complicated: The effects of complexity on conversations over potentially intractable moral conflicts', in *Negotiation and Conflict Management Research*, 21 July 2020. Available from https://onlinelibrary.wiley.com/doi/full/10.1111/ncmr.12192 [accessed 9 February 2021].

[13] Peter T. Coleman and Robert Ferguson, *Making Conflict Work*, 2015.

because I don't think it expresses clearly enough the right attitude or tone of voice. I have chosen to use the term 'interested questions' because I want to emphasize the importance of curiosity in conversation.

In a feedback session with a group of in-house facilitators with whom I was working, one participant asked another an open question: 'What is it you're not getting?' It may have been an open question, but the inference is obvious. Immediately, the mood of trust and support in the group changed, becoming temporarily defensive and awkward. The question was clumsy and the conversation shut down – which is the opposite of what was intended. Experiences like this underline the importance of planning for group conversations and having key questions prepared so they can be phrased helpfully. There are some questions you know you're going to have to ask, so think carefully about how to make them work for the listener before falling into the trap of getting the tone wrong.

The importance of open questions is emphasized in skills development or training sessions with good reason… but the lack of opportunity to fully embed how to articulate and frame them in practice can lead to muddle. This is a timing issue that arises because we need the time to think about what to ask and how to express it rather than diving in without considering the pitfalls first.

Poorly expressed open questions aren't interested questions. They bring the agenda back to the questioner. Here are some loose examples based on conversations I've heard recently:

- 'What would it be like if you were to give the client a call and persuade them to change their mind?'

- 'Why didn't you use the model I showed you?'
- 'Where should we run the session – I usually prefer to go off site?'
- 'When will it be ready then... Tuesday?'
- 'Who do you think is better for the pitch next month? Me or Nicole?'
- 'How's it going? I mean, I've heard it's a bit uphill so I'm getting a bit concerned about timings. Do you think we should push back?'

Arguably, the intention behind all of these is to ask an open question. But none of these is an *interested* question. They are all about the person asking the question and the opportunities to reply are narrow. The listener will know the inquiry is not about them or intended to benefit them in any way.

The answers you get depend on the questions you ask.
Thomas S. Kuhn

Here's a replay of those questions:

Open, but not helpful	Interested
'What would it be like if you were to give the client a call and persuade them to change their mind?'	'What's your view of the best way forward?'
'Why didn't you use the model I showed you?'	'Tell me about the model you used.'
'Where should we run the session – I usually prefer to go off site?'	'Where would you like to run the session?'
'When will it be ready then... Tuesday?'	'When do you think it will be ready?'

'Who do you think is better for the pitch next month? Me or Nicole?'	'Who's your suggestion for the pitch next month?'
'How's it going? I mean, I've heard it's a bit uphill so I'm getting a bit concerned about timings. Do you think we should push back?'	'How's it going?'

'Why' questions are tricky – they often carry an attitude of challenge or emotional undertone. It's easy for that 'judge' to appear! If you are using 'why' from a genuine place of curiosity, go ahead… otherwise, use cautiously!

In the flow of conversation, all these questions would lead to further probing before reaching a conclusion, but what's interesting to me is how easy it is to try to lead the listener towards a place that satisfies the concerns of the questioner. It's not about showing interest or opening up insights into what's going on for the other person. The questions are an expression of self-interest – a transaction that serves only one of the people involved in the conversation – the questioner.

It is important to recognize that skilful questioning is not simply a matter of starting a sentence with 'who, what, when, where, why or how'. Educator and philosopher Peter Worley[14] categorizes both open and closed questions as grammatical and conceptual. You might ask colleagues in a meeting, 'Have we got the right strategy?' it's a closed question, but a conceptual one, leading to an exploration of ideas involving all sorts of questions as the debate unfolds.

---

[14] Peter Worley, *100 Ideas for Primary Teachers: Questioning*, 2019.

A direct, closed question can trigger a powerful response that may start the conversation with energy. You might ask, 'Are you clear about what you want to get from this conversation?' The answer must be a version of 'yes', 'I think so', 'not really' or 'no'. Whatever it is, it's helpful because the next question can then be an expression of interest – you'll want to find out what's behind the response.

Let's define some interested question options:

Type of question	Helps the questioner	Helps the other person
Inquire		X
Funnel	X	X
Probe	X	X
Leading	X	
Multiple	X	
Loaded	X	
Recall	X	X
Rhetorical	X	X

You can hear examples of these questions in action in the listening resources section of the website:

www.listeningshift.com.

Going a little deeper

People enjoy being asked interested questions – after all, it shows curiosity in the questioner and gives us a chance to share our views, tell our experiences, give our opinion. You may want to use the TED acronym if you want the conversation to deepen and become richer.

T – 'Tell me…'
E – 'Explain…'
D – 'Describe…'

These starters are a great opportunity to get others to open up. They are especially useful if you find social situations difficult and land yourself in conversation with a person or group you've never met before and have to strike up a conversation and build rapport. The pressure to ask lots of questions can be inhibiting but the TED approach will encourage other people to speak at length. Then you'll have great material to help you ask follow-up questions.

Step 4: Interrupt mindfully

A note of caution on this one before we start. In 2018, Katherine Hilton, a Stanford University linguistics doctoral candidate,[15] conducted research on interrupting in natural conversation and found two distinct groups with opposing views on interrupting. First, she describes a 'high-intensity' group whose conversations are animated and where people speak easily at the same time. This group is less comfortable with silences. Then she describes a 'low-intensity' group, for whom two people speaking at the same time might be considered rude. She goes on to highlight gender differences in the perception of interruption, too. It's complicated and the rules of engagement vary, partly depending on culture, partly on context and partly on the familiarity of the relationship.

---

[15] Alex Shashkevich, 'Stanford researcher examines how people perceive interruptions in conversation', in *Stanford News*, 2 May 2018.

In the United Kingdom, Alan Robertson, the architect and founder of the VoicePrint™ profile,[16] positively describes a voice of challenge as one that interrupts to improve the quality of what is happening – a voice that refocuses the conversation. This might prove essential to move a meeting forward, so the context will be influential. But don't let that allow you to relax and feel that interrupting others won't matter in your world. The important knowledge is how you interrupt, if you must or do at all.

At the University of Northern British Columbia, psychology professor Han Li uses the following definitions in her research on cultural differences in interrupting.[17] Take a look at them and consider how you might interrupt others:

Cooperative interruptions

- Agreement – showing enthusiasm and support for the speaker's ideas.
- Assistance – if the speaker forgets a word or what they were about to say.
- Clarification – to check understanding.

Intrusive interruptions

- Disagreement – jumping in to voice a different view.

---

[16] VoicePrint Questionnaire, https://letstalk.voiceprint.global/about-voiceprint.

[17] Han Z. Li, 'Cooperative and Intrusive Interruptions in Inter- and intracultural dyadic discourse', *Journal of Language and Social Psychology*, 7, 35–46.

- Floor-taking – taking over the conversation but staying on the same subject.
- Topic-change – cutting in to change the subject.
- Summarization – paraphrasing the speaker's point and often minimizing it.

You'll see that the cooperative interruptions fit nicely with the concept of listening to support, whereas the intrusive ones carry more of a tendency to switch the conversation away from the speaker to satisfy another's agenda or solve it.

You may favour the high-intensity style of engagement in your meetings and conversations, and see it as a sign of engagement in the room. Notice *how* your colleagues interrupt, though. Is it to encourage or expose?

I've done a lot of work with a very high-profile and successful UK company. Full of energized, committed and brilliant people, presentation sessions are driven by interruptions, which have become a normal in-house style. Unfortunately, they are mostly of the intrusive kind. Ideas are shared by the presenter, who will barely have covered their initial findings before someone – often a senior stakeholder – will jump in to disagree, ask an off-topic question or 'take the floor' by sharing their own views on what is being presented. For people who don't like presenting, are junior to others in the room or who have not been given sufficient time to prepare, this is an unpleasant experience leading to anxiety about having to present, frustration in the presentation or, perhaps worst of all, apathy. What's the point of building an argument for developing an idea and preparing to present it with passion and enthusiasm if you're not going to get past the first slide and have it rigorously unpicked before you've had the chance to paint the full picture?

Unfortunately, intrusive interruptions are also a feature of defensive conversations, or those where conflicts need resolving. Rather than hearing both sides out, we interrupt to defend our view, to refute the allegation, to challenge the suggestion that we have done wrong. Emotions may be running high in these exchanges and these are the points at which we most need to engage the next step in our list.

Step 5: Acknowledge, encourage and appreciate

In all areas of my life – both professional and personal, I have noticed that conversations work best where there is acknowledgement and appreciation from both sides. It's a great way of building goodwill and an important way to let someone know that they've been seen and heard. It's much easier to have conversations with people who make us feel that they like us, recognize our value and are interested in building affinity and rapport. This 'easiness' is about bridging differences, collaborating and taking a long-term view of the relationship, the development of which may not feel easy, but is ultimately more valuable.

As an actor, I learned early that a play needs to be finished with a fully present curtain call. The audience applauds, sometimes cheers, sometimes stands in appreciation and the members of the cast return this acknowledgement with a bow, and often their own applause as thanks for the audience's warmth and attention.

As a coach, I am deliberate about encouraging and appreciating my clients for stepping outside what feels comfortable for them and exploring what's possible. If my role is to build confidence in new ways of communicating, how could I not offer specific observations about the new behaviours and skills I'm seeing adopted and implemented with success? If I do that well, I know that the next time I encourage them, they'll take even bigger leaps forward.

At Samaritans, we are encouraged to appreciate our callers for taking the step to contact us and to share important personal experiences. During those contacts, we reassure by encouraging our callers to keep talking if it helps. This encouragement is hugely effective – it's a way of showing that we want to listen, we are present and we care. Even in distress, somehow people are able to hear this encouragement and move forward. It's a powerful way of realizing the potential of encouraging words spoken in the right tone of voice.

Can you find a way in meetings and conversations of acknowledging the contributions of others? You'll be pleased to know it can easily be achieved. Something I've noticed in my observations of successful leaders over the years is their confidence in acknowledging the participation and contribution of others by making short public statements like 'I think that's right,' 'You make a good point,' 'Thanks for highlighting that for us' and so on.

I enjoyed watching a VP of marketing at a big international company skilfully get what he wanted in debates by deferring to the expertise of peers in the room. He would make comments such as, 'Of course, you've been so close to this and done such a great job… and I know you are way ahead of me in terms of expertise in this area, but I wonder if we could consider…' and then go on to introduce his own idea or initiative. It was mostly successful – people felt noticed, significant and appreciated. He knew how to raise a sense of status in his colleagues, making them feel important and taking all the threat out of the situation.

Status plays an important role here in helping others feel valued. This feeling enhances our sense of psychological safety in relating to other people, lowering any potential feeling of threat and raising our sense of reward. These are big tickets in helping people feel valued and recognized at work. And they are so easy to do.

Step 6: The sound of silence

I was tempted to leave a big gap in this section... lots of white page to demonstrate space. But I felt uncomfortable doing that – just as uncomfortable, in fact, as it can feel sitting with another person when no sound is being exchanged between the two. Silence may be golden, as the expression goes, and that may be true of some blissful quiet moments on your own somewhere lovely, but it's not a fitting description of the heavy canopy that descends when two people sit opposite each other during a painful or challenging conversation. Often full of meaning and emotion, the silence goes to the very heart of why listening can be hard. We may be afraid of what we are about to hear, and how we might feel when we hear it. In the silence, as we wait for what's coming, we can experience our own rush of emotions, and the desire to damp them down and fill the gap can be overwhelming.

Once you get used to silence, though, you begin to realize the immense value of it as a listener. You begin to relax – you don't have to drive the conversation but instead can wait for an offer from the other person. Just wait... they will say something – and probably something you didn't expect. There's a magic in sitting with another person in silence.

Solitary silent reflection can be transformative, but it can also lead to rumination, playing the same situation over and over again, losing sight of the facts or recreating them to serve our own narrative. Having another person there as we think requires us, when we are ready, to draw the themes together and find a way of expressing our thoughts out loud. Then we get a reaction, understanding and an opportunity to take our thinking to the next step – well, that's what happens if the listener is doing their job, of course.

What can you do to practise silence? Try these steps:

1. Notice how generous others are in giving you the space and silence to reflect in conversation with them. How do you feel if someone interrupts your flow of thought to give advice, ask diverting questions or bring the conversation back to themselves?

2. Confess to someone you trust that you're having a go at improving your use of silence. This might make you laugh at first, but that's fine. Take it as a bonus.

   Set up a five minute task in conversation – you can choose the topic, but it might be to ask them about their week, or something light where you can concentrate on the task, rather than worry about the content. Let them speak until they naturally finish – no interrupting.

   Before responding, count to 5. Ask whichever probing questions you are curious to hear the answer to. Let them talk again.

   Repeat using the count to 5 until the conversation reaches a conclusion.

3. Ask a trusted work colleague to join you for a walk. Invite them to talk about something that's on their mind and tell them you will be listening to them and

not interrupting, questioning or commenting. Tell them they have eight minutes in which to share their situation and thoughts about it. I know eight minutes is a long time… and what you can expect is that they will take a couple of minutes to share what's on their mind and then will run out of content. And that's where silence comes in…

Wait, walking side by side in silence. Without prompting, after 30 seconds or so, they will start talking and, during the next round of speaking, will uncover insights or share more deeply than in the first round when they were just setting the context. Keep going until you reach the full eight minutes. Then spend two minutes reflecting what you heard – more of that in steps 8 and 10.

4. Start to notice what happens to your conversations more generally as you deliberately use silence. Silence is a key factor in creating presence and developing gravitas – there's an output benefit to working with it. But the main benefit is to your listening. You won't get to be a great listener without finding silence. It will also give you the space to think about the next few steps.

Step 7: React

Sanford Meisner, an American actor and founder of the Meisner Technique,[18] defined acting as reacting. It's a simple

---

[18] Sanford Meisner and Dennis Longwell, *Sanford Meisner on Acting*, 1987.

principle that describes the importance of being present, with full attention, so that we are able to respond to any impetus we feel.

Reacting to what you hear is critical to the other person's experience of being heard. None of us wants to feel that we have been courageous enough to voice a view or share what matters to us, only to have it ignored or dismissed. Meisner's guidance is valuable because, if you are present, if you have given the speaker your full attention, you will have an impetus to respond and should express it.

Imagine the following scenario:

Colleague: That's it. I've had enough of all this. I've just spent two hours in a meeting on the presentation and no one can agree on anything, no one is listening – half the room are on their phones, the other half are just bickering about who's going to lead it. We don't even know who's doing what and, to top it all off, I've just had a message to say my car needs to be recalled and I haven't got the time to take it to the garage – I'm going to be here until at least 7.00 p.m. tonight and then I've got to head up to the Edinburgh office first thing in the morning. I haven't even got time to pack.
Manager: Oh, they'll be fine. Just leave them to it. I wouldn't get involved if I were you. I didn't know you were going to Edinburgh tomorrow! Any chance you could take some seasonal pictures of the castle for our social media team?

The colleague is having a bad day and is experiencing a build-up of small frustrations. The manager is trying to be helpful, but isn't listening. The manager doesn't want to talk about the meeting, isn't interested in the car problem at all and is thinking about their own agenda in relation to the mention of Edinburgh.

These interactions are a daily experience for all of us... they are a perfect example of well-intentioned, but terrible, listening.

The manager needs to *react* if they are going to demonstrate good listening.

Here are two phrases I find useful to show a reaction to what I've heard. Both are useful for showing a reaction, but not assuming:

1. 'That sounds...' – for example, 'That sounds like a terrible morning.'
2. 'That seems...' – for example, 'That seems to have built to quite a list of things to deal with.'

But the most important thing is to be in the moment, respond like a human being, and show compassion and understanding – show that you have noticed and that you care. Don't use it, as this manager did, as an opportunity to switch the conversation focus back to you.

Step 8: Repeat what you hear

Reflecting is a method of repeating back words or phrases that you hear the speaker using. It certainly helps to keep listening on track, as you are more likely to pay attention to the words you're hearing, but I confess to feeling awkward when I first discovered this as a listening step. It feels a bit mechanical and clunky – I thought it would make me sound robotic. But it works – it's transformative. Sometimes you can play back something that has just been said by the speaker and they'll exclaim, 'Yes! That's right!' almost as if they had no idea that the words had come straight out of their own mouth. That's a magic moment – your conversation has become a listening exchange.

This step is particularly useful when emotions are running high – difficult customer complaints, issues of conflict between team members or differences in opinion on the best way forward will all benefit from deliberate use of reflecting.

The manager could have repeated back, 'Sounds like you've had enough of all this,' which is a direct reflection of the first thing their colleague said. This phrase needs unpicking by the manager – it's a big statement and could be an indication that this colleague is thinking of leaving the business. If not being listened to plays a small part in a workplace relationship breakdown, reflecting as a listening tool is going to show that you are present and ready to engage in a bigger conversation.

Try it – you'll be amazed!

Step 9: Check your understanding

In other words, clarify what you've heard. Check in that you have understood what's being said accurately. It's acceptable to use a cooperative interruption to clarify because it's so important to understand exactly what's at stake.

There are two main risks involved in failing to check understanding – first as a listener and second as a speaker:

1. When listening, we can too easily fall into the trap of assuming. This is especially the case when people use

intrusive interruptions or try to switch the conversation back to their own agenda.

Try these signposting phrases to check your understanding:

- 'Let me check that I've got this right...'
- 'Can I clarify a couple of points...?'
- 'For my benefit, could we revisit...?'
- 'Let me interrupt you there – can I check...?'
- 'Let's take a pause and go over a couple of finer details to make sure we all understood the same thing...'

2. When *speaking*, we assume that we have the listener's full attention, when we know that this is variable at best.

Committing to clarifying little and often is another helpful method for staying present in a conversation – you will be listening out for signs and markers that need further investigation and you'll be saving time for everyone in the meantime.

If you are the speaker, give your listeners an opportunity to be confident that they understand fully before moving on or closing a meeting or conversation. Ask them to play back to you any points, reactions or thoughts that would help you know that everyone is clear. Make sure that this doesn't sound like a test by taking ownership for the process. Soften the challenge by suggesting you might have over-complicated, talked too much, covered too many points and request hearing things from their perspective as a means of ensuring that you are communicating clearly. Be sure to avoid the direct 'Are we all clear, then?' unless you can be sure that there is enough trust in the room to express doubt or uncertainty. Using habitual 'check-in' phrases with people – especially groups – can make us feel as if we have done our job of making sure everyone understands. The problem is that if your listeners aren't listening, they probably won't tell you. If they've listened and not understood, they probably won't want to share that with others in the room or on the call. And if they've half listened, and half 'got it', mistakes are likely to be made.

Finding a way to check understanding will be worthwhile for all involved.

Step 10: In summary

Our last step is to practise summarizing what's been heard. Just because it's the final step, however, doesn't necessarily mean saving it until last.

As a Samaritan, I have noticed that a person's story can take a while to tell – and that it will have many elements and characters, and often cover a long period of time. Waiting until the end of the story would be a big ask of my listening skills and put the caller under pressure to talk at length without being sure that they are being understood. Summarizing little and often is the answer.

In your meetings and conversations, it can be helpful to think in episodes and chapters. We'll go on to think about structure in Part Two, but in listening the practice of catching up as we go covers four things well:

1. It helps the speaker feel sure that they are being heard.
2. It takes the pressure off the listener to grasp everything that's being said.

3. It reduces the need for note taking, which keeps the connection and focus alive between speaker and listener.

4. It allows the listener to pick up on particular sections of the story to develop depth of understanding, rather than wondering where to start.

Summarizing also allows you, as a listener, to express what you've heard in your own words. This is a sure sign that you have not only listened, but also understood.

By now, your conversation is full of listening riches. You're really getting somewhere!

The listeners: The coroner

I asked senior coroner Joanne Kearsley how much listening matters in her work. She responded by telling me that a coroner's job can't be done without listening to people – not just in court, but also with staff and colleagues in the coroner's office.

Joanne began her career as a lawyer, so she is used to reading and understanding evidence before she hears it presented in court. This written material allows her to decide who she requests to give evidence, and enables her to pay close attention to and deeply understand the bigger picture as well as the details before she meets relevant witnesses. This, she says, is where she needs to listen closely to staff from her office, who will have spoken to family members and had to deliver and listen to difficult information. They will then feed in any concerns that need acknowledging and help her to understand the emotions of the bereaved.

Once in court, Joanne hears the evidence presented to her. This is the second stage of listening, having first gained understanding through reviewing the case files. She describes hearing the case as 'putting the jigsaw pieces into place'. Critically, this is where a coroner has to suspend judgement – the expectation and anticipation of how things may turn out can be very different when the case is presented by those closest to it.

She told me how important it is to keep an open mind – to check yourself. Jo feels you have to be strong enough to change your understanding – to admit that things may be more complicated than they first appeared to be. Her ethos is being there to help – by being proportionate and fair.

This is a perfect example of the importance of managing our inner judge, approaching the situation with empathy and listening to what is said – not what we wish had been said.

Coroners are required to deliver some of the most difficult and painful messages people will hear, often in regard to tragic outcomes, in highly emotional, high-profile situations. Jo feels that a key part of the coroner's skill in communication is helping people to listen. She is aware that the professionals involved may be desensitized to some details that could easily distress people connected to a case. Her focus is minimizing the potential for shock and damage to listeners, while ensuring that they understand fully.

Jo has learned to manage her impact, recognizing that not everyone will perceive her intention as she meant it. People are different, she says. You can't think about how you would do it – it's about them.

Setting your intention

If you've ever enjoyed a film starring the likes of Robert de Niro, Viola Davis or Michelle Williams, you'll have experienced an actor whose training was influenced by Russian acting theorist Konstantin Stanislavski,[19] whose method has been taught in drama schools and acting programmes around the world.

One of the principles of Stanislavski's work relates to a character's intention. His view was that in any play a character will want to achieve something, and by the end of the play we will have witnessed how they went about reaching their goal and what they encountered along the way. This overarching want is described in the method process as a character's *super-objective*.

Within the play, there will be acts and scenes, each of which will involve our character having an *objective*, which moves them towards their super-objective. Each interaction the character has with another character involves the playing of *actions*; these drive the scene and help the character reach their objective. These actions are not tasks; they are intentions. They inform how the lines are said – the voice, the body, the energy in performing the line.

It has always struck me how similar this is to situations that unfold in the workplace... As a CEO, your super-objective

---

[19] Konstantin Stanislavski, *An Actor Prepares*, 1936.

might be to increase your business profit by a number of percentage points. You will have objectives that work towards this and will involve the support of others. Each meeting or conversation you have will involve actions to help you achieve your objective. These actions will be how you engage and influence your listeners… the way you express your ideas, your conviction, your enthusiasm, your calm.

You'll recognize this as a way of looking at your strategy for influencing. I'll bet you didn't know that Robert de Niro might have thought the same way in preparing for an Oscar-winning role!

This is also a helpful way to think about meetings and conversations – it might seem like more detailed planning, but it will help you to set the tone for the conversation and ensure that you are present and clear.

1. What's your super-objective for the meeting or conversation? In an ideal scenario, what are you trying to achieve in your business or project at the moment?
2. What's your objective? What do you want to happen – or not happen – as a result of this particular meeting or conversation?
3. What's your action? What do you need to say and how do you need to say it to influence the other person successfully?

Actions take the form of an active verb: 'I [active verb] you'. They are what you 'do' to the other person to make them feel or respond in a particular way – for example, I worry you; I enthuse you; I caution you; I calm you; I rally you.

Here's an example:

- *Super-objective:* Reduce range offer and prior-itize best-sellers to streamline the business and increase profits.
- *Objective for this conversation:* Get Connor to feel safe and Aliyah to agree to timeline.
- *Counter-objective:* Don't get defensive about my decision.
- *Action (Connor):* Understand, support, reassure.
- *Action (Aliyah):* Understand, engage, challenge.

The same approach may apply when you are planning a presentation – particularly for an important interview or pitch – and can be a part of your process for helping others listen.

- *Super-objective:* Get the investment I need to build my product.
- *Objective:* Make them sit up and ask questions.
- *Counter-objective:* Don't ramble or bore them. No over-explaining.
- *Action:* Inspire, intrigue, convince.

I have lost count of the times I've had to ask a presenter whether the message they are delivering is good news or bad news because their intention is unclear. If you are working with a script, you can have as many actions as you like – slide-by-slide, line-by-line, explain each action, thus allowing your listeners to follow your emotional thread and keeping them present.

In a conversation, it is more about deciding on your energy, your presence – what atmosphere or emotional tone you set for the conversation.

Intention and commitment

I have drawn a couple of parallels in this book between an actor's process and the world of leadership communication. These techniques and skills are part of managing impact and being present.

The second part of this book builds on your intention and helps you to think about how to master the art of engaging your listeners by being clear, succinct and connecting with their wants and needs.

The listeners: The improviser

'The dance of communication' is how writer, director and improviser Dave Bourn describes our interactions with others. He believes we have to take responsibility – as a dancer does – for the follow and lead of conversation, during which 50% of the time we will be listening, and the other 50% is what we do with what we hear.

Dave describes improvisation as a creative process in which everything happens in the moment. Improvisation is distinct from other forms of acting and stand-up comedy in that there is no script, and no one knows what will 'be offered' by the other improvisers since nothing has been planned or rehearsed. To be successful, all improvisers must have maximum awareness and be 'in the moment', which Dave describes as when 'you stop thinking about what other people are thinking'. Interestingly, he came to improvisation to manage his own anxiety – something that benefits him as an improviser because he sees anxiety as a state of high awareness and reactivity to others. This experience essentially allowed him to become a listener by being fully present when noticing and responding.

As an improviser, Dave's attention is on making others look good. His intention is to be generous – not by trying to be funny himself, but by focusing on his fellow performers. His experience has taught him that by helping others, he will be helping himself. This is a process that ensures great theatre for his audiences, but also enables him to manage any anxiety or nerves by distracting him from his own thoughts as he strives to support his fellow players and engage with the audience interactively.

The art of improvisation lies in the balance between listening and speaking – this 'dance' of communication. If listening is the state of focusing on others from a place of heightened awareness, then what about speaking as an improviser?

Dave suggests the joy of improvisation is seeing something emerge completely in the moment. Anything can happen but it is *shaped* by the principles an improviser learns – for example, adding 'colour' as the essence of great stories. The colour is in the detail – using 'who, what, where, why and when' as a way of enriching the picture. Communicators get caught up on events and they don't fully engage the audience in the way these gleaming details do. He suggests focusing on the colour, and you'll make it easy for your listeners to stay with you.

Part Two

Shifting gear
Helping your listeners listen to you

The second part of the book looks at how to make sure you're not the only listener in the room. We'll address the importance of making what you say relevant to your listeners and the value of connecting your experiences with those of your listeners by being open. We'll also explore good technique that lays the foundations of ensuring that you are easy to listen to.

4

This shift means something
The importance of relevance

Where we think about the importance of crafting messages that are relevant for your listeners, focused on what they want and need to hear, not just what you want to say.

- The relevance gap.
- Three tools for relevance:
  - ○ A reason to listen.
  - ○ The magic of metaphors.
  - ○ Telling your listeners' stories.

Making communication relevant to your listeners

Personally, I am very fond of strawberries and cream,
but I have found that for some strange reason, fish prefer
worms. So, when I went fishing, I didn't think about what
I wanted. I thought about what they wanted.

Dale Carnegie[1]

Dale Carnegie's wise words make me smile, as a reminder that different people have different wants and needs. The quote resonates with me as a gentle prod that not everyone sees the world as I do.

It's not revolutionary thinking – we will all have had insights into our personality preferences through feedback or psychometric profiling during the course of our careers, and we know that acknowledging and embracing differences in preference or style is for the benefit of all of us – especially if there is an imperative to build diverse and inclusive teams.

But when it comes to communication, there is often a gap. Recognizing that we are wonderfully different doesn't

---

[1] Dale Carnegie, *How to Win Friends and Influence People*, 1936.

always translate into intentionally communicating in a way that is relevant to listeners.[2]

This is a problem: if communication is not relevant to us as listeners, then listening becomes hard work. If listening is hard work, the chances are that we will allow ourselves to be distracted by other thoughts that are *more* relevant to us.

The message is lost – and there may be a high price to pay for that.

The relevance gap

A few years ago I worked with a well-known UK brand that had been taken over by a US investor. The company was proud of the sense of community that had grown over the years and the business was full of passionate, committed and long-serving employees. I'm sure it was an attractive purchase from the investor's perspective.

Nonetheless, hard times lay ahead. Huge changes were rapidly imposed on the business, including significant restructuring, and many people were made redundant from the company to which they had dedicated their working lives. Emotions ran high – there was so much speculation about 'who was next'. The anger was pervasive: many people felt a sense of being excluded from relevant information; everyone seemed fearful and – perhaps hardest of all – there was a breakdown of trust in relationships as people jostled for position in an attempt to hold on to their job in place of their colleagues.

---

[2] Dan Sperber, *Relevance: Communication and Cognition*, 2nd ed., 1995.

The leadership team was aware that people were suffering and felt it was important to communicate what they could. It didn't work. Bitterness, gossip and in-fighting remained the order of the day for many months. The culture was changing – and not for the better. The longed-for uplift in profit did not succeed and difficulties continued.

How did it go so badly? Some of the answer lies in relevance. All communication was an attempt to explain what was going on from a leadership and shareholder perspective. The assumption was that colleagues would appreciate the commercial drive for the business: that they would be interested in the long-term vision; that they would understand the business needed to streamline and focus; that this meant shareholder value would increase.

Lengthy and frequent PowerPoint presentations were shared with management, who would then be responsible for passing on the plan for the future of this great company. Managers armed with swathes of information proceeded to share this new commercial ambition with their teams – often by reading out the information given to them – and Q&A sessions were shortened owing to the presenters' lack of any further information.

A burning need to know what would happen to jobs or how a role might look in this new world was not satisfied. The financial aspiration of the business and a rationale for action that would keep the business alive for the next 20 years was the only food on the table.

What do you think would have been relevant to the colleagues in the business? What was on their minds? How would you feel walking out on a 15-year career knowing that although you had lost your job, shareholder value would ensure a bonus in the years to follow for those lucky enough to have an investment in the company?

There is an important distinction here in our search for relevance:

1. What do people *want* to know?
2. What do people *need* to know?

The assumption made in this example is that people would *want* to know, where possible, what was happening and why. As this was of particular relevance to the leadership team, it was easy to believe that the same priorities would apply throughout the business.

In fact, there was a *need* for people to know how their lives were going to be affected, whether they stayed in the business or left it. Need is a powerful emotional drive that overrides any attempt to listen to what is being shared. Knocking at each person's door would be the agonizing question, 'What's going to happen to me?' Listening to anything else at that moment was just too difficult.

In this case, overlooking what people needed to know caused great difficulties – a culture of frustration, anxiety, apathy and denial grew by the day. Each successive communication approach was rejected by the listeners before it even began and, although rare, there was evidence of harm done by disaffected employees that cost money, time and goodwill, and caused some potential reputational damage.

Had the leadership team addressed the need that was so relevant to their listeners, everyone's journey through this necessary change could have felt very different.

The problem here was delusion – the leadership assumed they knew what would be relevant to their people and imposed it on them. They failed to consider what mattered to their listeners and made what they *did* share too hard to listen to.

If you are asking or expecting your people to make an effort to listen to you, you have to be sure that they will see the information you share as relevant to them.

Rules for relevance

Our starting point for any communication with anyone has to be by finding out what's relevant for them. This is empathy in action.

Challenge yourself:

- What do you think is relevant to your people?
- How have you built this view of what is relevant?
- What views, decisions and ideas are you imposing on people?
- Whose voices do you never get to hear at first hand?
- How can you find out what matters to them?

You might feel like this is adding to your already heavy workload – and it's risky saying to any leader, 'You may think you know what's relevant to your people, but I'm not sure that's true.' Both of those statements would certainly irritate me. BUT we know that problems with engagement exist in organizations. We know that time to probe and explore what really matters to people is tight.

Yet if we saw this investment in time to find out what people want to hear as a shortcut – a means to expedite messaging so that it was immediately meaningful and impactful, wouldn't it be worth doing?

Think of three people who are important to you. Try to identify people who are different – on the basis of gender, age, cultural background and so on.

Consider this statement: 'Climate change is relevant to all of us because we all live on the planet.'

This type of statement is intended to galvanize people into action – but it's an assertion. It may be true, but that doesn't make it relevant to individual listeners. It needs tailoring to allow it to resonate with different people for different reasons.

1. How might you recreate this statement to make it relevant to your three different choices of important people?
2. What angle would you take?
3. What examples would you give?
4. What language might you use?
5. What style of delivery would you choose?

Three tools for relevance

Your priority in making your messaging relevant for your listeners is to *ask* them what they want and need. This might be before you make a speech at a conference or a presentation to your customers or colleagues, or plan an agenda for a meeting. Ask... and listen.

If you don't commit to this approach, you risk becoming predictable in content and style. Predictable presentations and meetings are dull experiences that are way too much work for listeners.

Your job is to ignite a spark, light a fire and warm the heart. You can start this by using the following tools:

1. Give your listeners a reason to listen.
2. Identify metaphors that will connect to their experience.
3. Tell *their* stories to show that you have listened to them.

Giving your listeners a reason to listen

There are so many ways to do this, ranging from dramatic to conversational. The following is a useful list – you'll have other experiences and thoughts to add. The important thing to ask yourself always is, 'Why should they listen?'

1. Answer the question you know they want answered (ask them what that is first).
2. Make a shock statement.
3. Use humour.
4. Ask questions – rhetorical or otherwise.
5. Tell a story.
6. Offer numbers that are relevant to them.
7. Use media – video, music, images.
8. Share quotes.
9. Be silent – long enough to build anticipation.
10. Change the environment in which you communicate – be bold, creative and surprising.
11. Show a news headline.
12. Use props.

The magic of metaphors

Identifying metaphors that will connect to their experience

Metaphors are shortcuts that appeal to our emotions – allowing us to develop strong attachments and beliefs to an ideal and offering a shared language or means of defining a situation.

As an exploration of what experiences people are having in your business, asking them to use a metaphor could yield surprising and fascinating insights.

In *The Science of Storytelling*, author Will Storr[3] suggests that we use a metaphor approximately every 10–12 seconds of speaking or writing so they slip easily into our messaging and may be seized upon, repeated and developed as themes. This can be great – as long as it's relevant and intentional. If you choose the right metaphor, you can be sure it will be heard, recited by your listeners and planted deeply in the business. It's a quick route to engaging listeners, but because metaphors can be so powerful, you'll need to choose wisely.

Types of metaphors

In a crisis, we tend to apply war metaphors – to talk of 'being invaded' and 'going into battle' against the enemy. A quick glance through the commentary associated with the COVID-19 pandemic shows a litany of metaphors, similes and analogies associated with war and crime designed to provoke a

---

[3] Will Storr, *The Science of Storytelling*, 2019.

powerful emotional reaction in the public to encourage them to rally against the virus.

There are multiple ways of exploring and understanding metaphors and their potential for you to help your listeners. American fiction author Judy Blume[4] narrows a long list down to four key types of metaphor:

1. *Standard metaphors.* These are a way of describing a situation briefly and succinctly – for example, 'She is a walking encyclopaedia'; 'Your presentation is dynamite'; 'Love is blind.'

2. *Implied metaphors.* These involve subtle use of language to help us build a picture – for example, 'He roared at them'; 'Her eyes sparkled'; 'Drain the swamp.'

3. *Visual metaphors.* These create an association using images to compare one thing to another – for example, if you are talking about a challenge that is ahead, you may choose to represent what's being faced with a supporting image of bricks and scaffolding.

4. *Extended metaphors.* These build on a metaphor to draw out the theme – for example, using the mountain to talk about the climb, types of varied terrain and being at the summit. Be careful not to overdo it here!

Make sure you don't mix your metaphors so that people become confused. No 'hopping on the bus to soar like a bird in the face of battle to crest the wave as you finally reach the summit'!

---

[4] Judy Blume, 'Judy Blume teaches writing'. Available from www.masterclass.com/classes/judy-blume-teaches-writing [accessed 9 February 2021]. See also www.judyblume.com.

Commonly used metaphors in organizations

Some metaphors pop up time and again in business communication. The intention is positive, and I appreciate the decision to try to engage creatively. The problem is that when we hear anything used repeatedly, it tends to lose its power and stops being relevant. It's not that it is hard to listen to, it's just dull… and dullness is a sure and certain off-switch for relevance as we stop listening and switch mentally to another, more interesting subject.

The examples I've heard most commonly are:

- *Going on a journey*. It is all too easy to rely on the listener knowing exactly what you mean by a 'journey'. This is an opportunity for a truly sensory narrative, but what tends to happen is that the communicator relies on the single word 'journey' to do the work, without extending the metaphor to build a compelling vision.

- *Climbing a mountain*. While this creates a compelling mental image for the listener, it is a difficult metaphor to use if you want to create positive engagement. Not many people have climbed a mountain and those who have often tell amazing stories of life-threatening challenge, freezing and alone in terrifying conditions with little oxygen. It's not necessarily the picture you might want to provoke in listeners facing an immediate challenge.

- *Going into battle*. The intention here is to create a sense of community fighting together, fellow troops united with a common purpose. But war is dangerous and casualties are many. It can be a risky metaphor to 'deploy' if your aim is to engage and unify.

- *Sport.* I have worked with many leaders who seek to use sporting metaphors, often because they have their own experience of team or individual sport involvement that has inspired them. It can work, but it can also exclude a large part of your listening audience because it just isn't relevant to them. Your personal story is interesting... but if you are asking your listeners to metaphorically scrum in the freezing wet mud, you'd better be sure they share your knowledge and enthusiasm.

- *Mixed metaphors.* Combining metaphors is confusing, and can lose the listener and weaken the message. Trying to cover enough ground to find relevance for everyone ends up losing them all instead.

Recently, the metaphors I've seen used in print and social media seem to be changing. I detect a movement from a strategy of push to a tactic of pull – engaging the heart, using a compassionate mindset, demonstrating empathy for people.

You may want to play with unifying metaphors – building bridges, drawing maps, shaping futures. Positive and optimistic visions of a sustainable world; homes, not houses; communities, not cities; nurturing and supporting, not driving and chasing. Metaphors that show ethical, moral, values-driven leadership.

You have to pick up on the zeitgeist and satisfy your listeners by showing that you share their concerns, that you have listened and that you understand what is relevant to your community.

Telling your listeners' stories

There will be riches in relevance throughout your business – wonderful examples of strategy in action, culture, overcoming adversity, challenging the status quo and so many others. They are out there – you just need to find them.

You can connect the stories you hear in your business to any major subject or theme and make it relevant to your audience. For example:

- Do you have year-end statistics to share? Tell a story about what these numbers mean for some of your colleagues and customers personally. What's changing – for good or bad? What will satisfy the burning questions they need answered?
- Is there a new strategy? This will affect the lives of everyone in the business, so tell stories about the evolution of the strategy – how it started, how it developed, who you want to thank in your business for its inspiration and evolution.
- Do you have product success to share? Tell your audience about the working lives of people in the plants and factories who make your product. Bring that community into the room and connect everyone to them.

Don't feel like all relevant stories have to be ground-breaking, high drama or revolutionary tales. There is relevance to be found in everyday, personal micro-experiences and fleeting moments, and sharing these will show just how committed you are to being connected to your community.

How to tell someone else's story

We have a responsibility in recounting the relevant experiences of others in our businesses to tell the story well enough to make it a low effort listening experience. This needs skill and confidence. What makes someone else's story come to life? Try the following:

1. Remember that a good story is like a stunning and varied landscape – plenty of peaks and troughs make it fascinating to observe. When you hear a story that you know is relevant to your people, work out what the highs and lows are in the story flow and work around them. A nice way to practise this is to reflect on the life of a person you know well and list three high points and three low points you know they've experienced. Think about how you'd build a narrative around those events… and that's it. You're already prepared to recount a compelling and engaging version of their life's experience using the contrasts they've encountered.

2. Bring the characters to life – if you've ever referred to a customer, or used a job title in your stories, you're missing a trick. Any old customer, bank cashier, nurse or baker is not going to be relevant to your listeners, nor will they powerfully resonate with them. But if you name them (real or otherwise), and tell us that they're a grandparent, sister or son with values we may share and struggles we understand, you will be accessing the details that make relevance happen – we feel affinity and connection with people whose

lives mirror our own in some way. Consider including the following:

- their name
- their stage of life
- their family circumstances
- how they sound when they speak
- how they look
- their attitude to life
- how they relate to your business.

3. Include tiny details – pick one or two moments in your story sharing that bring the narrative to life with the kind of details that make the experience real:

- Describe a room, or location in close detail so that we can visualize it.
- Describe what someone is wearing in detail.
- Describe an object in detail.

Above all, keep the conversation going – ask for input and feedback, and reflect and review as often as you can to be sure that you are keeping the content of your conversations and presentations relevant for your listeners.

5

This shift is hard
Show the struggle

Where we recognise the value of sharing personal challenges, journeys and transformations in inspiring others. Unscripted, in-the-moment communication that creates energy and connection.

- Build your book of relevant stories to share.
- How to tell your story.

The value of sharing stories

Bear with me. I am not suggesting that you live out an anxiety dream of standing unprepared in front of your colleagues feeling exposed and humiliated as they wait, wide-eyed on the edge of their seats, to see what will go wrong next.

Far from it. The struggle to help others listen is about presence and impact, fully supported by preparation, rehearsal and technique.

At RADA, as I learned to improvise, I also learned that watching someone 'struggle' in performance was captivating. Seeing a performer strive for the right words, to find the right moment, to seek the connection onstage to create magic with a fellow actor allows the audience to take part in and bear witness to the struggle. It's captivating stuff – it feels fresh, spontaneous and immediate.

I suggest that embracing the concept of struggle positively will help others listen for two reasons:

- Stepping away from scripts, slides, board papers or rigid agendas can inject energy and presence into communication as you struggle, or strive, to find the right language and tone to engage your listeners. We'll talk more about this in the sections on structure, music and vocal dynamics.

- No one sails through life without a struggle. While this may have created difficulty at times in your life, hearing about it will make you very easy to listen to.

Listening to the struggles of others is compelling – it is a privilege. You will be opening a window on your values and motivations, making your purpose meaningful for others to share. It's your own version of the hero's journey – you start out, face adversity, overcome it and return home transformed for the better.

Struggle is full of intensity – communication just at the edge of discomfort. It is exciting, unpredictable, real. That is always compelling to listen to.

Nonetheless, some of us are happier than others to open the private doors to our world, and it's important to do this in a way that feels right for you. As you reflect on the options below, be sure that you are comfortable with the examples you decide to use and that you will feel at ease emotionally about sharing them.

A note of caution – this will work brilliantly but ONLY if you are committed to careful planning and preparation, and rely on the good techniques we'll explore here.

How to tell your own story

Build your book of relevant stories to share

I can guarantee you that when you are talking to people across your business about what is relevant to them, what they say will strike a chord with you – it will trigger memories, stories, anecdotes and examples from your own experience that will be helpful to share, in order to show that you have listened and to help them listen to your priorities in return.

It is important to be prepared. Treat yourself to a dedicated notebook – I think paper is more helpful as the act of writing thoughts longhand seems to help them to stick. Jot down anything that comes to mind that could be useful. The following list may enable you to file your ideas, providing categories that will mean you can choose a relevant experience to share when you need it.

The following categories are inspired by Annette Simmons, in her book *The Story Factor*.[1]

- *Who are you?* Your listeners will want to know who is in the room with them – stories about you, your

---

[1] Annette Simmons, *The Story Factor: Inspiration, Influence and Persuasion through the Art of Storytelling*, 2019.

influences, your background and what has inspired you.

- *What have you done?* Your listeners will want evidence that they can trust you... what can you tell them to demonstrate that their working lives are in safe hands? How have you come to this point and what have you done to prove yourself?
- *What motivates you?* Your listeners will want to understand your values – not necessarily related to work, but rather the leadership ethos that will guide them.
- *What's your purpose?* Your listeners will be curious about how you will lead them into the future – following a purpose, a vision, a mission.
- *How do you care for people?* Your listeners will need to hear about the experiences you have had in your life that demonstrate how well you understand theirs.
- *How do you bounce back?* Your listeners will want to be inspired by knowing how you overcome adversity, which will inevitably raise its head from time to time – what did you learn?

Useful plots around which to build your stories

In his book *The Seven Basic Plots: Why We Tell Stories*, Christopher Booker[2] presents an analysis of stories and their themes influenced by Jungian archetypes. I have chosen four

---

[2] Christopher Booker, *The Seven Basic Plots: Why We Tell Stories*, 2019.

that you might find helpful in telling stories of struggle to inspire your listeners:

1. *Rags to riches*. The classic Cinderella story works brilliantly if you're trying to inspire your listeners to believe in possibilities or recognize how far you, or they, have come. Have you ever started from scratch and made a success of something? This is a story that will uplift your listeners and help them to see the power of transformation.

2. *Overcome the monster.* Any James Bond afficionado will tell you that there is nothing more compelling than a story of seeing threat and striking it down. These rollercoaster energizers will bring your listeners onside and help them to see how you deal with challenges. Have you ever felt fear? Experienced self-doubt? Lost sleep worrying about a situation? Sharing what happened to bring you to where you are now will help your listeners feel they are in safe hands with a leader who has learned from experience.

3. *The quest.* No excuses are needed in Hollywood to turn a story into a series of films when a quest is involved (think of *The Hobbit, Raiders of the Lost Ark*...). Starting a story with a vision for how it ends is a classic approach to engaging listeners with purpose. This is a story full of struggle as you jointly navigate the ups and downs, and support each other. It's also a way of keeping the story evolving over time, and one that may be co-created by all involved.

4. *Rebirth.* One of my all-time favourite films is *Groundhog Day*. The story of a man who relives the same day over and over again until he learns to be a good person is a

perfect example of a rebirth story plot. But what about you? Have you ever repeated a mistake? Have you repeatedly taken the same approach to solving a problem until one day you realized you simply had to find another way? This plot is a great way to inspire a desire for change in your listeners, and your experience of it will build confidence in them that you know how to lead them through it.

How to tell your story

Sharing your struggle is a fast-track route to building credibility for your listeners. You are making it easy for them to listen to a compelling story that they may identify with, helping them realize that you understand them, relate to their experience and that you care enough about them as people to open yourself up and introduce who you really are. This generous act alone is making your messages relevant, and therefore easy to listen to.

The great thing about telling your personal stories of struggle is that you hold the keys to the door, which you can open as much or as little as you like. However much that is for you, here are three encouragements to include to keep your listeners on the edge of their seat:

Give them the last line first

Decide what the last line of your story is and start with it. Then tell the story and then finish with the line again. Don't explain the line or carry on past it. Think of it as the wrapping around a box.

Use the senses

Using sensory description is a trump card in personal story-telling. As we listen, we trawl through our memories to make a connection to what we hear – for example:

> The head teacher is a small woman with crisply lacquered white hair. She wears an academic gown that billows around her as she strides through the freezing corridors of my school. Her voice is controlled, but cuts through chatter like a single high note from a saxophone – piercing, insistent, penetrating. She smells of mints. To shake her hand is surprising – it's warm, pudgy; it rests fleetingly on mine without any attempt at a squeeze or a shake and is withdrawn quickly.

This is a description of the headmistress at my secondary school. I can see her in my mind's eye so clearly – and you probably have your own picture of her in your mind as you read. But the truth is, our images will be different. Yours will be informed by related experiences from your own memory… it doesn't matter. It's a connection – an engagement.

For a moment, as we are thinking back to our school-days, you and I are in the same place.

It's easy to rely on sight as the primary sense in our narrative building, but the other senses add riches to the detail and build a fuller picture, making your stories even easier to listen to. The five senses are: sight, sound, smell, taste and touch.

Try this exercise on your own or through facilitation with a team or group. You might want to let your mind wander or write down your thoughts and revisit them over a period of time. Whatever approach you choose, try not to rush... let the sensory experience unfold until you feel you've really 'got it'.

Set a date – for example, five years from now.

Imagine you are walking into your business with a prospective or new client.

- What do you see? Detail the picture as richly as possible: What's the location of your building? What type or size of space? How is it laid out? How many people are there and what are they doing? What colours do you see? Lighting? Natural light? Height of ceilings? What else can you see?
- What do you hear as you enter the business? Music? Technology? Conversation? Silence? What else?
- What smells do you notice? Coffee? Fresh air? Essential oils that set the mood? What is distinctive? What else?
- How do you feel? Calm? Energized? Do you stand or sit in this space? Does it feel pristine, relaxed, welcoming? What else do you notice?
- What can you do in this space? Is it for meetings? Can you eat here? Can you draw on the walls? Interact with avatars? Print designs in 4D? What's possible?

> Dare to dream in this exercise – the richer the sensory picture, the more you will enable people to listen, engage and envision their future in your business.

The moral of the story

Whichever approach you choose to tell stories that enable your listeners to connect and commit to action, there is one thing you must include – always: the point of telling the story, or its moral.

A well-told story that is easy to listen to needs balance. It also needs to help us in some way – to transform us because we have listened to it. The moral of the story is your opportunity to teach your listeners something that will spark change, to inspire them to think, feel or behave differently as a result of hearing the journey shared in the story.

Unfortunately, this message may easily be lost if the story is rambling, poorly structured or, critically, doesn't have an end point that makes sense to the listener.

Decide what this end point is before you embark on sharing your story… then you know where you're going and why you're heading there.

It can be helpful to announce that you are setting up the key point of the story. Try one of these:

- The moral is…
- Why am I telling you this…?
- The take-away is…
- Here's the point I'd like you to remember…

Some 22 years after its first conference was held, TED Talks launched online in 2006. These 18-minute presentations changed the game in communication and enabled millions of bite-sized learning experiences for people who were now able to access them anywhere, at any time. Story-driven to engage and inspire learners, the TED approach meant that communicators everywhere were expected to do better than just read data from a slide. They needed to become storytellers.

TED Talks make their content relevant for listeners. They are full of struggle, there are sense-driven stories in all of them and they are structured, crafted and rehearsed. TED speakers know how to make their content easy to listen to – and they always have a point of transformation at the end – a moral of the story.

Making sure you have that in place as you speak will ensure that your listeners are hanging on to the end of the story as it unfolds, and that they get it. They get the point... and they'll take action because of it.

Helping us listen: The journalist

Local news journalist Emma Elgee knows that helping her readers engage with the stories she shares is about making the story relevant. She told me that the key is to get the human voice in as soon as possible, that we are fascinated by people's stories – we want to know someone's point of view.

Importantly, this means that, as a journalist, you have to get out of the way. She is clear that when you are sharing a story, however good your writing is, your job is to make the language accessible. This is not about dumbing the language or content down, but you have to be able to reach all readers – any and every person that engages with the story needs to 'get it' to ensure that they continue to read. Using jargon or unfamiliar, complicated terminology and language turns people off and the opportunity is wasted.

If the objective is to engage and sustain a reader's attention, then a good headline is a place to start. This, it appears, is a skill in itself. Some national tabloids pride themselves on sensationalizing a headline, but Emma counsels against this, preferring to allow the story to develop from a clear headline without over-promising. This, she says, is where a person's voice offers value – if you can use a quote in a headline, the drama is provided for you and the personal narrative has already begun.

Journalists rely on key questions in building a story – who, what, why, when, where… and 'so what'. It's the 'so what' that unlocks the emotion – the question that helps us understand the meaning. Asking the question 'So what does this mean to you…?' connects immediately, leading to heartfelt and sincere insights.

Emma advises against too much context – tempting as it is to develop a story into a full history and background, her view is that this interrupts the flow as the detail is not always relevant. Where possible, she advocates for the use of a single sentence and a focus on being concise.

Finally, she says you have to be able to change the story focus – be prepared to find a new angle. For that, you must be willing to listen… you can't be sure of what's going to unfold, and you have to be prepared to change your approach to the story. You have to really pay attention to be sure you don't miss anything.

She has some simple advice on helping others listen:

- Boil your information down to a single nugget. Ask yourself, 'Why would anyone care about this? Why would they need or want to know?'
- Get the story impact in straight away – a relevant voice that connects with people will do far more for your message than anything else.

6

You've got this shift
The importance of technique in helping others listen

Where we are reminded of the value of investing time, effort and attention in communicating with skill, using planning structures for presentations and conversations, using the voice to convey intention and emotion, and creating a listening environment.

- *That shift needs structure.*
- *Music – your voice matters.*
- *Choreography – creating a listening environment.*

That shift needs structure
Presentation and conversation planning

One of the words I hear used most often in relation to exceptional communication is 'effortless'.

The dictionary definition is 'requiring no physical or mental exertion' and 'achieved with admirable ease'. Sounds wonderful. In relation to helping your listeners listen, this would seem to be the vanguard.

Perhaps you enjoy watching comedians fluently navigate a two-hour set of hilarious insights and commentary on the way we live. Maybe you feel drawn to TV interviews with high-profile interviewers seamlessly interrogating the professional and personal lives of their subjects. Perhaps you've admired motivational speakers mastering the stage and commanding the attention of their listeners as they recount stories of triumph and draw parallels with business life. All of them unscripted, spontaneous original speakers... effortless.

Of course, as with so many things in life that appear to be easy, the truth is a little different.

The difference begins with structure. The more structure you use as you plan to communicate, the more likely it is that your listeners will be able to hear what you've said and understand it. With the comfort and support of your structured planning, you will be able to speak freely, knowing that you've enabled your listeners to stay with you. Here's why:

1. You will know exactly what it is you want to say and can be sure you'll say it.
2. You'll use fewer words and more pauses in between content to allow the listener to absorb the message.
3. You'll appear certain – this inspires confidence in the listener, making them want to hear more.
4. You'll know how you're going to end the presentation, or conversation. This gives your content a sense of direction and purpose.

The important message to underline here is that structure is not rigid, and it's not using a script – both these things will stop people listening as much as rambling might. It's about clarity, brevity and simplicity.

Let's think about helping your listeners listen in two key areas: presentation and conversation.

Presentation

Whether in person or online, presenting is part of business life. Since Robert Gaskins and Denis Austin from Forethought Inc released their PowerPoint presentation programme in 1987, slide presentations in business have become ubiquitous. More than 30 years later, we are still wrestling with how to use the medium effectively. Snapped up by Microsoft 3 months after the programme's release, it seems clear that the value of visual aids was recognized as a game-changer in helping people connect to content and remember information. And it doesn't seem like this will change any time soon

– a poll of MIT MBA students in 2017 suggested that 85% of them felt their ability to present – and use PowerPoint to do so – was a meaningful part of their role in business.[1]

But does a PowerPoint presentation help your listeners listen? It depends… and a good deal of what it depends upon is how you structure the presentation and slide content.

Does *this* look familiar?

I'm going to make a guess here – it won't apply to all readers, but many of you will have built a presentation for your listeners in the following way:

1. You decided what you needed to say.
2. You started to build a deck of slides from a template.
3. You added content – to ensure you didn't forget anything.
4. You asked for input from a colleague or senior stakeholder.
5. You incorporated their additional content.
6. You added some images.
7. You added any notes at the bottom – source references, explanations, etc.
8. You put in a slide at the end saying 'Any Questions?'

Maybe – if it was a significant presentation – you used a specialist provider to design slides and you may have walked through the presentation with them to see whether any

---

[1] Kara Baskin, '3 surprising ways Millennials communicate', 2 October 2017. Available from https://mitsloan.mit.edu/ideas-made-to-matter/3-surprising-ways-millennials-communicate [accessed 10 February 2021].

amendments needed to be made to the words on the slides. And then maybe again – probably the day before – you might have done a walk-through with the slides on the stage. At this point, you may have discovered that your content was really hard to remember fully, so you added a few extra bullet points to help. You also jotted down notes on cards. You might have felt very anxious and wished you hadn't agreed to present.

Unless you were presenting online, of course. No problem there – you could just read from your script. There was no need to run through the presentation beforehand – you could just turn up and it would probably be fine.

Where is the listener in all this?

Waiting for inspiration, for change, for the leap of emotion that says, 'I know what I have to do and I'm excited to do it.'

On the day, you felt exposed – a bundle of nerves. You just wanted it over and done with. There were a lot of 'blanks' in your head because of nerves, so to be on the safe side you read what was on the slides and tried to expand on the points where you could. You finished the presentation with relief – but because of the cortisol running through your system, you couldn't remember what you'd said. You overran by 10 minutes, but no matter – you got through it.

Yes, you did.

But without the listener. You lost them when they realized you were reading out loud; when they sensed you would be overrunning, encroaching on their coffee break; when they couldn't follow what you were saying because it was so hard to know where you were heading.

Perhaps this scenario doesn't apply to you... but there are many companies where this is entirely reflective of what happens. It's not effortless, either. It's full of the wrong sort of effort – effort that serves neither the speaker nor the listener.

It is a wasted opportunity for everyone involved.

A starting point for structure

To make any message easy to listen to, we need to know *exactly* what it is we are trying to say – *exactly* what it is we want people to hear and remember.

Before you plan any presentation, challenge yourself to decide how you would deliver the whole thing in one seven-word sentence. The rules are:

- It's a sentence – not seven random words.
- Prepositions and articles are included in your word count.
- Anyone would understand it – no business jargon, just plain English only!

This is a great route to starting to present with a focus on helping the listener listen and to mastering structure.

Before you try it with a business message, have a go at the following exercises, which are more of a fun way to realize that every story – and every message – has an essence from which you can build.

Easy practice

Think of a favourite film – anything that springs to mind will be suitable. Try to summarize the story of this film in one seven-word sentence. There are some rules:

- Focus on the story of the film.
- Don't include the title, catchphrases, actor names or character names.
- Don't use the phrase 'A film about…'

Here are three examples to start you off:

1. Wrongly convicted banker escapes jail through sewers.
2. Shark kills beachgoers, is hunted and shot.
3. Wicked stepmother loses stepdaughter to dancing prince.

There will be many ways of summarizing these famous stories, but you can probably guess which they are… *The Shawshank Redemption*, *Jaws* and *Cinderella*.

Harder practice

Start by watching one of TED's most viewed presentations – Daniel Pink's 'The Power of Motivation' – and see how you might summarize it in one seven-word sentence.

Apply the same rules:

- Focus on the overarching *story* Pink shares.
- Don't use the title of the presentation.
- Don't use the phrase 'A presentation about...'

Think about the last three presentations you had to make – it doesn't matter what size of audience you were communicating with. See whether you can summarize the story of the presentation in one seven-word sentence.

For example, I might seek to translate 'Enhancing our customer-centric mindset by focusing on core competencies' to 'Offering brilliant service with a simplified range'.

Once you are sure you have your core message, you can build it out using the following structure.

A structure to lean on

The structure I'm using here is built on Aristotle's principles of persuasion, which are well-known and acknowledged essentials for recognizing how to balance a message – especially in presentation – that ensures people are able to listen.

The principles are:

1. *Logos*. This is appealing to the listener's logic or reason. In a presentation, it means artful use of structuring your argument and providing supporting evidence.

2. *Ethos.* This is demonstrating your character or personality. I describe this as showing the listener who you really are, conveying your expertise and why they should listen to you as having credibility in the subject.
3. *Pathos.* This is emotion. Your ability to affect how your listeners feel is key here. If you demonstrate emotion, they will be more likely to feel the same – which is the root of charisma.

Logos lends itself to a classic interpretation of presentation structure. I've used this with clients for many years and it's my favourite 'go-to' planning tool – an amazing shortcut to allow me to prepare an easy to listen to presentation in seconds, if needed.

The structure

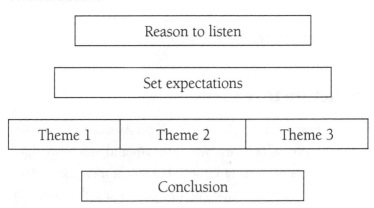

I find this approach universally useful. It works well when planning:

- a full-day meeting or training session;

- a presentation of any length;
- a structured answer to a question.

The following sections provide more detail.

Reason to listen

We know this is the key to establishing relevance for your listeners and it needs careful thought. Try not to make this the presentation heading... That's simply not enough to make the job of listening easy. Be creative, brave, open and challenging here – anything that provokes an emotional reaction will do the job – as long as you can make it *relevant*.

Set expectations

Briefly, tell the audience what's coming. Presenters spend far too long on this and listeners get lost in an endless agenda list – a guaranteed way to lose them. Use these few sentences to tell them what the purpose is, how they will feel as they hear it and how long you'll take. Then dive in.

Three main themes

The more I work with the principles of helping a listener listen, the more I realize that the key skill is not about what content we put into a presentation... but what we leave out. We almost always give in to the temptation to oversupply our listeners with information. Choose which three areas need focus or are the priorities for this particular presentation or message. This will make sure that what needs to be heard will be.

Note: If you decide what you want to say and then walk away from your planning, try to recall everything you've decided upon. Chances are that whatever you can't recall will be the stuff you're not really connected to, and if you can't remember it then it may be that your listeners won't either. This may guide you in your decision about what to leave out or use at a later date.

You'll need to discipline yourself when you are presenting to stay in the theme that you are discussing. Don't dot about!

Conclusion

After your discussion with your listeners, avoid ending with 'any other questions?' There's nothing in that statement that tells me how I should leave the room feeling, or what I should do as a result of listening to you.

Challenge yourself… do I want action or reaction? Maybe both… but use the opportunity to define this thought at the start of your planning process. Then you'll know where you're heading as you speak.

And your listeners will leave having heard – and remembered – the most important part of the message.

Alternative structures

Of course, this is by no means the only way to create an easy to listen to presentation. There are certainly alternatives, and a wealth of literature is available on how to master them. I offer you this structure because of its flexibility and application in so many communication situations and because Aristotle's influence lies at the foundation of so many approaches to structuring stories, plays and film scripts.

The important thing is to recognize that using a structure in message delivery will help people listen. If they're listening, you're doing your job and doing it well.

Structuring a conversation

Change happens one conversation at a time.

Most of this book is a call to listen in conversation more than we speak. But a conversation is a dialogue, so it is critical that you are able to manage the psychology of the conversation and represent your ideas and convey your messages in a way that enables listening.

As Nancy Kline said,[2] 'The quality of your attention determines the quality of another person's thinking.'

The exchange matters – we need a balance of expressing what we want to say, while enabling the other person to have the same experience.

Often in leadership, conversations are about managing challenge. This might be to fulfil a vision, agree refreshed values, manage a sharp growth. But it's just as likely to be about the tough stuff – performance management, increasing workload, reorganization and sometimes letting people go. Conversations that might be a difficult moment for a leader may be some of the standout moments of the listener's life – a conversation they never forget. So let's make sure those conversations are remembered for the right reasons.

---

[2] Nancy Kline, *Time to Think: Listening to Ignite the Human Mind*, 2012.

Must do's

First and foremost, you need to get the essential message across to the listener.

Second, you need to know they've understood it. This is not about saying the same thing over and over like a broken record. It's about taking responsibility for the way you articulate the message. If they don't understand, that's on you – not them. This should make you work harder to think of ways to help – to serve your listener so that they are clear.

Start by asking yourself these three questions before you decide how to structure the conversation, as far as that's possible:

1. What do I want to happen?
2. What do I *not* want to happen?
3. How do I want them to feel?

How to give a perspective so that the listener hears it

You can take two routes to structuring a message, depending on its nature and who it's for.

First, you can go down the route of contrast – this is a straightforward route to clarity with an evident emotional journey, leaving the receiver in no doubt about the request but also feeling valued.

- Get straight to the point.
- Offer an appreciative route forward.

Second, you can plan how to set the scene for the conversation using the following model (*Note:* This is an outline plan and *not* a script. You can hear this in action in the listening resources):

I like...	A positive appreciation of the other person's efforts, qualities, intentions, etc. can go a long way towards relaxing the conversation at the start, making them feel safer and more receptive to listening. You can afford to provide detail here – as long as it's both sincere and specific.
I don't like...	You now have the legitimacy to raise an issue – but only one. Don't use this as an opportunity to compile a list of irritations because you will lose the listener, who will then feel attacked. Keep it clear and brief.
I feel...	Own it – what's the impact on you? Don't use 'I feel that you...', but rather 'I feel X emotion.'
I want...	Go for it – in one sentence, tell them exactly what you want going forward.
If you do...	These are positive consequences – the potential outcome if the new behaviour or change is adopted. This should include what's in it for them as well.
If you don't...	These are negative consequences – the likely outcome of not taking action. Include what they can expect if they are unwilling to move forward.

How to say no so the listener hears it

We know by now how important it is to work on empathy and understanding the perspective of others. If you've done a good job on thinking about that, or are naturally empathetic, you might find saying no hard to do. The problem is that if we avoid saying it clearly, the other person may not hear it at all. If you have no problem saying no, I encourage you to think about how you express it – this is an example of when a message can be too straightforward, causing hurt and offence when none may be intended.

Instead of just coming out with it, try the following structure:

Acknowledge the feelings of the other person.	It's important to prime them for the impact. Make this your own, but test out statements like 'I know this is difficult to hear' or 'I've given this a lot of thought…' or 'You might be disappointed by this…'
Give them the message.	'I'm going to say no'; 'It has to be no'; 'Unfortunately, it's a no.'
Explain why it's 'no'.	Limits need to be applied here. One reason *only* is sufficient – more than that, and we lose the impact of the message or confuse the listener.
Offer a route forward.	This could be an alternative suggestion or an offer of support or resources, but see whether you can think of something that eases the other person away from the disappointment of hearing 'no'.

A general rule about structure

The point of structure is to use it to enable fluency. It frees you to be present and 'in the moment' rather than worrying about what's coming next in your presentation, which example you can remember to demonstrate your competency or what you should say or ask to move the conversation forward.

Any structure tool might feel a bit awkward or clunky in the first instance, so test them out to find the language and style that fits you.

A shift in responsibility

I have often encountered leaders who are frustrated by a lacklustre reaction from their listeners. They may receive feedback showing that the listeners don't understand, don't feel motivated by what they've heard or are reluctant or resistant when it comes to taking action. This often results in complaints from the leader… irritated by people's lack of engagement and disappointed by signs of apathy, the tone turns against the listener.

In fact, the responsibility lies with the speaker… it's our job to make the information clear, memorable, inspiring. If they missed the point, that's on us.

Ask yourself, 'What could I have done differently?' Ask *them* what they would like done differently and how you can help them listen well in the future. Painful though the feedback may be, it's what will allow you to make a difference and grow as a communicator.

The following sections will help you dive deeper into reaching your listeners with imagination and a touch of individual magic.

Helping us listen:
The political speechwriter

Senior adviser George Leigh faces the challenge of articulating ideas persuasively in speeches that must convey urgency and drive change. He told me:

> There's a commonly recognized metaphor in political speechwriting known as the 'Dog Show Speech' idea. If a politician, celebrity or local business leader has to go and judge a dog show – and make a speech before announcing the winner – they can't use it as a platform to talk about what's on their mind. The audience is there because they're interested in dogs. You have to talk about the dogs – you have to give the audience what they want.

Sometimes the purpose of the speech is to be critical – but the people in the room won't want to hear that. George tells me that you have to find a way to win people around. You can't attack – your listeners will switch off. It's important to create an ongoing conversation. It takes a lot of work.

The priority in any speech is to say something. You must have – and make – a point. Tony Blair's speechwriter, Phillip Collins, says that point should be clear enough to put on a post-it note.

George describes listeners as 'indulging you'. They're being generous with their time. He feels you shouldn't be rude to them by wasting their time or failing to help them understand the point.

He starts with the title, thinks about who is listening and then does his research and receives a full briefing. There's a tendency in making a speech to fill space – he aims to get rid of what doesn't matter and fights to keep the time tight, suggesting 10 minutes is about right.

Sometimes, he says, you have to be patient with semantics – because language matters. There can be a lot of debate about the differences between using the word 'target' versus 'goal' or 'aspiration', for example. But the overriding thing is that it has to be the language and tone of the speaker – their voice. It takes a lot of conversation and background work to understand how a particular speaker would say something. It has to be right for them – they're the one saying the words.

George uses a few rhetorical devices – taking care not to sound pompous. He believes the music of the speech is very important. He thinks of the grammar as musical notes – the cadence, the crescendo at the end. His view is that if you get that right, the speaker doesn't have to be the best speaker in the world – the way the words have been written should carry them so people can listen.

Music
Your voice matters

I first started working with leaders on communication and executive presence in 2000. At this time, a piece of research was being quoted in almost every book I read for inspiration and every article I sought for evidence on the subject.

In the late 1960s, Professor Albert Mehrabian produced a paper on his research into non-verbal communication.[3] The study involved a woman saying nine single words and adapting her body language and voice with each delivery. Participants in the study would respond to what they saw and heard, and Professor Mehrabian noted what they relied upon in making their judgement. The main finding was that when there was incongruence or inconsistency between the word spoken and the voice tone or physical gesture, participants relied more on the non-verbal interpretation than the actual word. The findings produced an accessible and memorable statistic – 55% body language, 38% voice tone, 7% words.

Perhaps because this statistic was so easy to understand, it became the 'go to' reference for how people should consider their impact in communication. You can still come across it all too easily in a Google search, in articles and in

---

[3] Albert Mehrabian, *Silent Messages: Implicit Communication of Emotions and Attitudes*, 1972.

books on communication today. Presentation skills, conversation training and coaching in executive presence quoted this 'rule' and encouraged clients to focus exclusively on the non-verbal aspects of their communication. This was never Mehrabian's intention, though, and the findings absolutely did not suggest in any way that we need not consider the impact of what we say.

If you've worked through this book in a linear way, you'll know that what you say and the structure in which you convey it provide a route to enabling others to take in information and remember it with ease.

You may remember or have read about the efforts Margaret Thatcher made to lower the pitch of her voice to make her more appealing to listen to. Thatcher recognized that her listeners identified a lower, masculine tone as being the voice of authority – of power. Research has found that this remains the case; in common with animals, we seem to hear a low tone and confer higher status on the communicator.[4] This is an interesting effect that is particularly relevant for women in leadership as they seek to engage listeners.[5]

Here's what we know:

- In social situations, and with babies or young children, both men and women will raise the pitch of

---

[4] Deborah Tannen, *You Just Don't Understand: Women and Men in Conversation*, 1992.

[5] Casey Klofstad, Rindy C. Anderson and Susan Peters, 'Sounds like a winner: Voice pitch influences perception of leadership capacity in both men and women', *Proceedings of the Royal Society B: Biological Sciences*, 14 March 2012. Available from https://royalsocietypublishing.org/doi/10.1098/rspb.2012.0311 [accessed 10 February 2021].

their voices. This might be an unconscious attempt to lower our status and to connect without threat, by building rapport with those we encounter.

- Both men and women with lower-pitched voices are perceived as more competent than those who speak with a higher pitch.
- Higher pitch voices in women are perceived as more attractive, but less competent.
- A wider pitch range use in the voice is perceived as more engaging in both men and women, but is perceived as carrying less authority.

This is all interesting information, but perhaps it is more important to bear in mind that your listeners won't like anything that they sense is an inauthentic sound. If you try too hard to lower your voice to convey authority, you might be perceived as 'faking it', and you will lose your listeners straight away. Margaret Thatcher might have had to take a different route to crafting her vocal authority now than she took in 1981.

We have to remember that human beings tend to prefer a voice that is not extreme – a 'normal' sounding voice is genuine, relatable and trustworthy. There may be things to pay attention to that manage distractions for your listener, but be careful not to move too far away from the real you.

Key considerations

Pause and silence

The section on the application of silence in listening in Chapter 3 showed its value as a tool to encourage others to go deeper, to reflect, to share more of what's on their mind.

Silence plays its part in speaking too. It's the music, the punctuation, it's what allows our listeners to reflect – to soak up what they've heard and interpret it. It can take courage to pause, but it's where magic happens.

The celebrated playwright Harold Pinter is famous for his exploration of pauses in his plays. He uses three different types:

1. *Ellipsis*. Represented in the text by three dots, this pause is a hesitation, which may be only slight.
2. *Pause*. This is used when a character is deep in thought. It's compelling for the audience to feel the atmosphere tense as we wonder what is going to happen in the space in which we are held.
3. *Silence*. A dead stop – the character has encountered something so absurd that they can find nothing to say. This is equally compelling for the audience and can have a chilling effect of raising our stress levels as we watch the drama unfolding.

Pinter was determined to write dialogue that reflected how people really communicate in life, which he did to great effect. We can learn so much from him about using silence to build atmosphere, and have your listeners on the edge of their seats as they wait for what they might hear next.

The place where you have the most chance to experiment with pause and its power is when you are chairing a conversation, updating a team or organization on significant issues, telling a story or making a presentation. Anecdotally – and from personal experience – I suggest you have a lot longer than you think. Ten seconds is not too long if you want to emphasize a really important point. The trick is to allow the listener this time, but you have to appear comfortable with it yourself.

Note: Online, you will need to keep some form of slight movement – for example, hand gesture, slight movement of head – to land a pause so that your listeners don't think your screen has frozen.

A strong accent

Accent can cause other people to form impressions of so many things about us – ethnicity, class, gender, cultural preferences and education, to name a few examples. There are more than 30 dialects in the United Kingdom, and with as much as 20% of the world's population speaking English – many as a second language – the chances of hearing English spoken with a standard English accent are limited. That's what makes English glorious, but as listeners the English speaker from the 'inner circle' of countries that are native speakers (linguist David Crystal's definition of countries in which English is used as the primary language)[6] can be quick to judge. The linguist Vivien Cook[7] notes that second language speakers experience a bias against them that is not included in unconscious bias training and are disadvantaged 'by the gap that still separates them from the "ideal" native'.

If you have an accent, celebrate it for conveying authenticity and all the incumbent history and riches it contains. At the

---

[6] David Crystal, *English as a Global Language*, 2nd ed., 2003.

[7] Vivian Cook, 'Monolingual bias in second language', *Revista Canaria de Estudios Ingleses*, 34, 35–50 (1997); see also Monika Schmid, 'Accent prejudice is costing people the jobs they deserve', *Quartz at Work*. Available from https://qz.com/work/1741578/how-people-judge-you-based-on-your-accent [accessed 10 February 2021].

same time, make sure that it's not so strong that it allows your listeners to switch off from your ideas and messages because they find an accent too difficult to understand or follow.

Use simple terms, examples and stories in a well-structured message and you will give yourself the best opportunity to enable listeners to stay with you.

A good way of mastering awareness in this area is to get feedback from a range of listeners who you trust to be honest and specific. You may also record yourself as a means of recognizing what your listeners are hearing when you speak; as a support mechanism for understanding the feedback you receive; and as a starting point for making changes that you can measure through repetition. There are readily available resources online to help make any minor adjustments needed to transform a strong accent into an accessible one. Alternatively, invest in some coaching support.

Paralanguage

This is a 'catch-all' term for anything that isn't words and includes the music or pitch of the voice, the pace and any habits that form part of the way we speak. Become aware of anything that might distract from the simplicity or power of your messages and try to manage it more effectively.

Filler sounds

Filler sounds – for example, 'um' or 'err' – provide natural spaces to allow us to think in conversation. They are useful as long as they are not ubiquitous. They are described by linguists as 'discourse markers', and in conversation are a demonstration of politeness or consideration, softening the impact of a message or allowing a moment for listeners to reflect.

If you have been on a speaking or presenting skills course, the likelihood is that your attention will have been drawn to any such habit. While these sounds have a place in our spoken messages, they can – under pressure – amplify as our mind speeds up and our rate of speaking increases. I don't ever advocate for complete eradication of filler sounds, as this can make us a bit robotic in delivery – it sounds like we are scripted. And on the phone, filler sounds can be an indication that you are still thinking, so they can be useful.

Ask someone for feedback on any distractions related to overuse of filler sounds or repeated words, because they risk stopping others listening. Be helpful in your request for feedback in this area by asking specific questions that will give you the insight you need.

Pace

Particularly online or over the phone, you'll need to pay attention to pace or rate of speaking. Adaptability is important if you are going to effectively hold the attention of your listeners. In the case of pace, one size doesn't fit all. I know it can feel clunky to rethink an aspect of your communication that has felt instinctive for as long as you can remember, but the more you pay attention to it, the more natural it will feel to adapt and the easier it will be for your listeners.

	One-to-one	One-to-few	One-to-many
Fast (more than 160 words per minute)	Fine	Limit/vary	Avoid
Medium (120–160 words per minute)	Fine	Fine	Vary
Slow (100–120 words per minute)	Fine	Limit/vary	Limit/vary

Note: This is a guide to reflect on your skill in adapting. Situation or context may change an approach entirely: you just have to pay attention and decide what's appropriate or enabling for your listeners.

A tip: If you want to find out your natural rate of speaking, use a transcription app (e.g. Transcribe, Otter or Rev) to record your voice in conversation, then copy and paste a section of the conversation into a Word document to get the word count. This will give you a starting point from which to practise adapting pace.

Word choices

In 1929, German American psychologist Wolfgang Kohler[8] found a correlation between two nonsense words and two abstract drawings. The words were 'Maluma' and 'Takete'. One drawing was angular and the other curved. When asked, the majority of participants chose the angular drawing to

---

[8] Wolfgang Kohler, *Maluma and Takete*, 1929.

represent the word 'Takete' and the curved lines to represent 'Maluma'. Many studies have replicated this effect around the world and the majority find a similar correlation. Why does this matter to your listeners? To make an impact vocally, to underpin the music that enables them to pay attention, you might want to be very intentional with certain key word choices.

In English, consonants carry the conviction of the language (perhaps the best evidence of this is to consider the impact of swearing, which is often short words that begin and end with consonants and a single short vowel in the middle) and vowels carry the emotion.

Imagine you are communicating with people in your business and you want to help them understand a significant change – perhaps a rise in the number of customer complaints. Which of the following words might you choose:

- spike (definition: a sharp increase)
- surge (definition: a sudden large increase)?

Try saying these words out loud and test the impact they have on your delivery. Subliminally, your word choices will make a difference to the listener.

For famous and influential figures in public life, key messages are written by experts and then rehearsed until the speaker is comfortable with and confident about what they're saying and how they are saying it. They concentrate not just on what messages to deliver, but which words will drive those messages into the hearts and minds of the listeners and stay there. With thoughtful effort and attention to the words you choose, you can significantly improve your impact on your listeners.

Helping us listen:
The voice coach

Andrea Ainsworth has been voice director at The Abbey Theatre in Dublin since 1995 and is one of Ireland's leading voice specialists.

In our conversation, we talked about the use of the umbrella term 'soft skills', applied to development in communication skills. We agreed that the term suggests a lack of rigour, precision or methodology, and that it's not a good term to use if you're trying to encourage people to dedicate themselves to improving – the phrase is somehow undermining.

As an expert in her field, Andrea is often asked for 'tips and tricks' to help people get better in communication when her view is that these are skills that should be approached as an athlete might approach getting better at their sport: by using dedication, focus and hyper-awareness, alongside being open to feedback, reviewing your performance and taking a long view of reaching excellence. These are not quick fixes.

Andrea describes listening as a quality of attention – the hyper-awareness of what's going on inside you and around you, and feeling the connection of others. This interplay allows you to respond in the moment with what is needed. She was clear that if you operate in a culture where people don't really listen, they won't be able to change the way they speak – or much else.

In helping others listen, Andrea focuses on the use of silence. She counsels that pausing, even for a beat, allows the listener to process what has been heard. She has noticed that nervousness can lead speakers to add too much detail or technical information, while fear of interruption can lead them to not finishing points and having no new vocal energy for the next thought or point. Encouraging people to work on how they shape an argument and to practise this enables shifts or changes in the way the speaker articulates their thoughts. Without the music of language, expression lacks finesse and is too hard to listen to.

Andrea's advice is to do the following:

- Hear what has been said – and not your version of it.
- Anxiety to fix makes us look for a problem to solve. Try to just 'be' with someone – this is the translation of a phrase she learned in her Feldenkrais training, which was 'Etre avec quelq'un'.
- Think about how you 'place' yourself. Online or face to face, the environment we are in affects the quality of our attention, and what people see in front of them affects their response.

Vocal dynamics

In 20 years of working with individuals and groups on communication skills, I have never met a single person who says they love the sound of their own voice. Recording a speaker in conversation or presentation and playing the recording back to them usually results in exclamations of dismay: 'Oh, I hate my voice! I sound all nasal/whiny/like my Mum or Dad/such a strong accent.'

The problem is one of recognition. We hear our voices conducted through bone and muscle. The tiny ossicle bones in the middle ear vibrate as a filter to manage the sound we produce, which would be much louder without this filtering process. Our voice is deepened as a consequence, which is how we hear it.

When we speak, the voice travels through air – producing the very different sound that is heard by others. What we hear recorded is pretty much what everyone else hears – and that can prove surprising and uncomfortable. Of course, the more practice you have in recording yourself, the more familiar your voice or sound becomes. This allows you to become adept at making necessary adjustments to convey the appropriate emotion you need to influence your listeners.

Voice is muscle – and, as we all know, a well-exercised muscle is strong, flexible and responsive. Fortunately, the voice is a willing instrument and it doesn't take much work to keep it in shape or get the most from it.

The VAPER model

When you speak, your listeners need two things from you:

1. Intention – for you to be completely clear about the emotion driving you and the emotion you hope to engender in them.
2. To hear your voice as a free, flexible and ready vocal instrument that does your bidding and inspires them.

You have all you need to achieve those two things.

Here are the five aspects of voice that offer us an opportunity to adapt and improve so we are easier to listen to:

1. V – olume
2. A – rticulation
3. P – itch
4. E – mphasis
5. R – ate

Volume

Audibility correlates with credibility. How can you expect your listeners to listen if they can't hear what you say?

Online

- The volume advantage online is that we are all projected at much the same level – if someone is too loud, we can turn them down. Softly spoken? Use a headset or microphone and you will be easy to hear. It's a real positive in our communication toolkit.

- The volume disadvantage is sound quality. Poor connection or too many people speaking at once makes things difficult to hear.

Be sure your listeners are able to say how easily they can hear you. If it's repeatedly difficult to listen, they will switch off.

Face to face

- Position yourself where you can be easily seen by everyone in the meeting or presentation.
- Avoid looking down at your notes – your voice will be difficult to hear if it is directed to the table or floor. Maintain eye contact with your listeners and the direction of your voice will follow your gaze with more energy and strength.
- Try not to think too far ahead, as your current sentence or thought will tail away in volume.
- Sit up – you'll need to be able to breathe well to get maximum power in your voice.
- If you need to interrupt, use the other person's name to get their attention before you do so – expect to have to repeat it two or three times if they are in full flow.

More than 40% of the UK population aged over 50 years has hearing loss.[9] It is therefore likely that some of your listeners may struggle to hear you. Get feedback from trusted

---

[9] RNID prevalence estimates using ONS population data 2018.

colleagues on how easy you are to hear and understand, then you can take action if you need to.

Articulation

This is the term for our level of speech muscle precision and energy. If you want to speak with authority for your listeners, you'll need to put some energy into your word formation. I think this work is fun... but it can feel a bit silly. Tongue twisters and pulling shapes with your tongue, lips and face might feel daft, but it does the job of toning your speech muscles so you express yourself with clarity, confidence and conviction.

Practice tip: Take a work document or slide presentation – something with lots of words and phrases relevant to your business. Read a minute or so of it out loud as fast as you can, but also as accurately as you can. If you make a mistake, go back to the beginning. Make every word precise. This is a bit more sensible than a tongue twister, but if you're happy to do one of those then Google is a rich resource in all languages.

Pitch

Music, colour, range, cadence and engagement all fall under this heading. Babies and children are hugely expressive with their pitch range. As we get older, this reduces until our age can easily be identified by our voice owing to the reducing flexibility in the muscles that support the larynx (unless you keep working at it, of course!).

Practice tip: Count from 1 to 10, alternating each number from the highest point in your pitch range to the lowest – for example, 1 = high, 2 = low, 3 = high, 4 = low, etc.

Emphasis

Emphasis is the process of doing the work for the listener – helping them to understand your intention. This can change the meaning of a sentence – a classic voice exercise is to place emphasis on different words in a sentence to see how the meaning changes.

On the phone, or when using voice only, it's the only real chance we have to help our listeners understand how they should feel about what we say, where the urgency is, what matters.

Practice tip: Try saying the following sentence emphasizing the word printed in italics each time and see how the meaning changes and is conveyed by your voice:

I didn't move them.
I didn't move them. (It was someone else)
I *didn't* move them. (I left them where they were)
I didn't *move* them. (I just covered them up)
I didn't move *them*. (I moved something else)

Choosing the emphasis on four different words results in four different sentence meanings. Part of the problem in written communications is that a lack of emphasis leaves the reader to infer the intention, and confusion or upset can sometimes result. Don't let that happen with your spoken voice.

Rate

As we have discussed already, rate is the foundation of pace in a voice. Use of pause and pace of speaking constitute the big ticket in voice use, so if you concentrate on nothing else, get used to adapting your rate to hold your listeners' attention and guide them as you speak.

Choreography
Creating a listening environment

Paying attention to the communication environment goes a long way towards making sure that people are able and available to listen to you. You are responsible for creating the conditions that help your listeners listen.

Imagine you are driving through the most breathtaking scenery you've ever experienced – a winter drive through a stunning, mountainous landscape with glacial lakes, endless blue sky, bright sun. It's 3°C outside and the crisp, cold air heightens the brightness of everything you can see. And then imagine that your car's heating system is broken – you have another two hours of driving and you are freezing cold. How fully are you able to concentrate on the beauty you can see around you, and how much of your awareness is focused on how uncomfortable you are because you are hunched over the wheel trying to keep warm and not really achieving your goal? Your attention will be split at best. Your inner need to be more comfortable will override your wish to appreciate what you can see. It's an inevitable inner conflict when our environment is causing us to be distracted.

Creating a listening environment that helps your listeners to listen is a way of being kind to yourself and them – giving everyone the chance to be at their best for the experience.

Face-to-face: Presenting

Take an honest look at the space in which you plan to present. Use fresh eyes to appraise the lighting, the seating, the layout of the room. What can you do to make it better, more comfortable and offering fewer distractions?

Then decide how you will choreograph your presentation delivery... sitting, standing or a bit of both? Where is best for you to position yourself so that you can easily be seen by everyone in the room?

Actors are taught that centre stage is the position where you can look forward and see everyone in your peripheral vision without having to turn your head.

This is a great tip for presenting when sitting down, because we are often poorly positioned, which means we have to work really hard to be seen by everyone around the table. If we don't make it easy for people to see us, they'll switch off and do or think about something else.

Face-to-face: Conversation

When you're clear about the type of conversation you want to have and what you want to achieve from the conversation – as well as what you don't want to happen – you can decide which environment will help and how to create it. Whatever you do, make sure it is clear to the other person that this is a listening environment – laptop closed, phones away, table or desk clear of distractions so that there is space for them to sit comfortably and sense that you are fully present.

Think about where to sit in relation to the other person – sitting opposite each other with a desk in between is mostly perceived as creating a barrier, so check in with yourself to see whether it is going to affect the tone of the conversation and what alternatives might be available or helpful.

Online: 10 must-do's for helping your listeners in online communication

Choreography for online communication requires us to be even clearer. We are responsible for setting the scene for our colleagues online so they have as few distractions as possible. Mostly, at the moment, I see people just 'turning up' with very little thought about their impact. Here's a 10-step checklist:

1. Invest in equipment that helps your listeners see you and hear you as clearly as possible – a camera and a microphone. These can be bought quite cheaply and can make a massive difference.
2. Lighting – don't be lit from behind, or the side. You will need to face a window or ring light so that your face can be properly visible to your listeners.
3. Connect your computer via ethernet cable. Currently, relying on WiFi in presentation or conversation is not adequate or reliable enough. Key parts of what you say may be missed and while interrupting to check or clarify because of a delay in poor connection is okay once or twice, after that people stop bothering.
4. Stand up as often as possible – especially if you are presenting. Your energy will be much better and if you usually feel uncomfortable standing to present, this will liberate you. You will feel much more comfortable when you return to face-to-face presentations.

5. Check that you are about a newsreader's distance from the camera – that is, when they are sitting. Make sure you are framed from the waist or chest up: don't let your face fill the screen. Research shows that a face in close up as the image on our screens tends to raise our subconscious feeling of stress owing to threat.

6. Make sure that your eye level is level with the green or blue light next to the camera lens. You must be at eye level to create a positive impact in conversation. Looking down the lens is intimidating for the other person and creates a difference in status.

7. Invest in a second monitor so you can see everyone on the call.

8. Keep your camera ON. Make sure you can see yourself at all times – this is a fantastic opportunity to learn about your impact. You can monitor your facial reactions, how energized or present you appear on camera to the other person. In a conversation or presentation, this is the best auto-feedback you'll ever get.

9. Set the scene at the beginning of the conversation – tell the other person where you are and what they can expect. For example, if you have a habit of looking away – out of the window, at the floor, doodling – and will therefore frequently look away from them, tell them to expect this; otherwise they may think you are distracted or disinterested. Warn them of any potential interruptions that might occur. Check your background – make sure it sets the scene you want it to set and is less fascinating than you are... we are all done with fake backgrounds. Frame yourself

authentically, but think carefully about your background and what it is saying about you.

10. Turn off all other potential notifications. Having a conversation where we can hear emails coming in, texts being received or WhatsApp messages flooding in is distracting for all parties involved. It tells us that there are other things going on, and we are not being fully listened to.

Noticing your listeners' reactions

The problem with being distracted in communication is that it can stop us noticing. If you have done your utmost to choreograph the environment to minimize any of the distractions that might get in the way, you will be free to pay attention to the subtleties and nuances of voice and body language that will give you essential information about how the message is landing.

You'll be operating in two environments:

1. *High context.* In the room with your listeners, you'll be able to rely on a rich sensory picture to tell you how things are going. Facial expression is an obvious one… but it's far from the only one. Widen your gaze to look at the 'dance' being played out.

   • *Hands.* Clenching or gripping, fidgeting or hidden, the hands will be a good starting point for your insight. Look out for the hands 'comforting' the speaker as they use one hand to stroke the other or touch their neck repeatedly. Women might also play with their hair.

- *Feet.* A real giveaway. A person may appear very calm in their upper body, but the feet might be telling a different story. Check for fidgeting, tapping, shuffling, rolling onto the outside of the foot. Are the feet 'locked together' – a sign of discomfort? Or are they splayed out, taking up space and appearing relaxed?
- *Body posture.* What does a person's overall posture tell you about their energy for the conversation. Are they upright? Rigid? Slumped? What information can you glean about your colleagues' readiness, commitment or general emotional state?

2. *Low context.* Online with your listeners, you'll have much less data to observe (which is why it's so important to make sure to be as clearly visible as possible), so facial expression, voice and words play a much more powerful role.
   - *Facial expression.* Pursed or tensed lips are a giveaway of tension or disagreement. Check the smile, too – a genuine, or 'Duchenne', smile involves the eyes. A smile that relies on the lips only is sending a polite message that looks more like an obligation than engagement. People who are feeling uncomfortable or awkward will often lick their lips in response to a dry mouth. This is a sign of stress, so tread carefully.
   - *Eye contact.* This is tricky online as we are not able to make direct eye contact at all. One person may be looking at the camera, but they will not be able to pay close attention to the other person on

screen. Both people may be looking at the image on screen, which is not making eye contact. Use this indirect gaze to pay close attention to the image in front of you and see what you can infer from the general picture.

What to do with what you see

Say what you see – and *only* what you see. This takes courage and practice, but it can unlock a conversation and make it meaningful really quickly. Honesty in this situation will help you both.

Say *exactly* what you've observed: 'I notice your lips are pursed and I'm wondering what might be causing that.'

Be careful here! Don't interpret – for example, 'You're looking cross and you're obviously upset about this situation.'

Use of 'I notice…' is helpful. It shows you're paying attention and it will help raise the awareness of the other person. Since the evidence is in front of you both, it may speedily lead to a more open conversation.

> *Presence is connecting with the thoughts*
> *and feelings of others.*
>
> **Rudolf Laban**

Helping us listen:
The choreographer/director

Denni Sayers is one of the leading operatic chore-
ographers of her generation and is internationally
acclaimed for her work. She considers staging from an
audience perspective *and* what the experience will be
like for the performers, describing the importance of
understanding the symmetry or asymmetry of a scene,
teasing out what will best tell the energy of a moment.

She describes a priority in staging as 'balancing
the focus' – leading the eye of the audience to where
you want them to look.

In rehearsal, it is likely that Denni will have 65 to
85 chorus singers in a room who she will never have
met. She needs to hold their attention for the duration
of the rehearsal, to inspire them to work well together,
to challenge them to learn new skills. She needs them
to value the movement as highly as the music.

She believes the key to this is preparation.

First, no matter the numbers involved, she
learns every person's name from photographs. This
helps the group to recognize that she has prepared
fully and, crucially, that she cares about the people

as individuals rather than as 'a chorus'. If you treat people like sheep, she says, they'll behave like sheep. Addressing people by name helps them to feel seen and ensures they will go the extra mile.

Second, she makes sure she can speak their language – learning the music as well as they know it. Denni told me, 'If I'm expecting them to dance and sing, I think I have to be expected to know the music *and* the dance.'

Third, she shared the motto 'You only make a first impression once' as a key principle in driving preparation. Her focus is the first 15 minutes of any meeting, which she sees as key to success. Her experience of groups is that they make up their collective mind really quickly and once you've lost them, it's really hard to get them back. Denni advises assuming the best of people as a route to getting the best from them.

Finally, she shared the value of knowing your material well enough that you can easily improvise if your plans are clearly not going to work. She is unafraid of things going wrong – drawn to the acronym FAIL as an inspiration… 'FAIL' stands for 'First Attempt In Learning'.

Her advice on helping others listen is to:

- get the focus of the room right – ensure that what needs to be seen and heard is available to everybody, and
- use humour – it relaxes everyone so you can do more.

7

Shift happens
How to take care of yourself as a communicator

We all spend most of our working day communicating – listening, talking, writing, reading. In this book, I have asked you to intensify your commitment to doing this well – to reflect, to practise, to review and to try again. It's exhausting stuff... imagine if you had to learn to walk differently? Something we take for granted that is so instinctive becomes draining as we unpick our process to improve on technique, develop style and inspire others to make the same changes. Not easy.

On the final pages are some tips for managing yourself as you embark on these changes... and a reminder of why it all matters so much.

- A note of caution as you listen well.
- Kindness.

A note of caution as you listen well

I am writing this book as we approach the second phase of lockdown in the United Kingdom. I am in Portugal, facing two weeks' quarantine on my return to the United Kingdom. I feel generally anxious and I am worried about family and friends – worried with a persistence not typical to me. It's a nagging sense of unfinished business and uncertain future.

I'm a good listener – you'll be pleased to know, as you reach the end of this book! This means that people reach out to me often. And, because I am committed to listening, I also ask questions. I inquire, I dig a little deeper. I have become less afraid of what I might hear, less afraid of how I might feel when I hear the difficult stuff. At the moment, in this restless time of social hijack, I am a useful friend to have.

This morning, I noticed that I felt drained. The news is depressing, I had an exhausting weekend organizing the logistics of moving location with my daughter and I hadn't slept well. I took a long walk to try to settle myself, but the phone rang and the walk turned into a long listening exercise to the caller. I ended the walk feeling more drained than I had when I started it. You may identify with this common experience, and it's useful to notice the impact before it morphs into frustration expressed in another later conversation, probably with someone else.

I feel reminded of how important it is to look after yourself as a listener. Here's a non-exhaustive list of options that may help you avoid the weight of listener burnout:

- Observe the shift principle... you'll be listening all day, so try to think in shifts and take breaks.
- If there are days when you're not 'feeling it', be honest where you can and ask to reconvene the conversation. It's rare for everyone to be 'available' to listen fully at the same time.
- Identify a colleague who is a good listener and agree a 'co-listening' shift where you can listen beautifully to each other in the spirit of reciprocity without seeking advice.
- Recognize that excellence ebbs and flows. Be kind to yourself – you won't always get it right.
- Manage your energy! Coffee, sugar and crisps are magnetic beasts... but they don't help our energy as sustained listeners.
- Find a bit of silence for yourself. You're going to be using a lot as you pay attention to others, but don't forget to use it to pay attention to yourself.
- You will need to carve out space to breathe... deep, energizing lungfuls of fresh air that give you energy on the way in and take the tension away as you breathe out.
- Save some of your listening skill for those you love... don't burn yourself out listening to people at work and then use your 'downtime' to avoid paying attention at home. If you manage yourself well, your skills will enhance all areas of your life.

Kindness

July 2012
Presentation coaching session: 08.30–10.00hrs
Location: London
Client: Investment analyst
Time: 09.55hrs

'I think I've lost my confidence,' he says, looking at me over the large spare expanse of desk that sits between us.

I wait, looking at him.

He gets up and walks to the window. The view is wonderful – stretching over the river to the other side of the city. His arms are crossed, his feet planted.

We are both deep in thought. I am wondering what on earth to say to this powerful man. Tall, good-looking, seems invincible. I have no idea what's going through his head. It looks like something significant, but I don't know how to go there.

'I've been thinking about my family,' he offers after a really long pause. 'The business – you know. Everything.'

'Go on,' I say.

'Ahh, it's probably nothing. I'm tired – just need a coffee and get back to it,' he says. The energy shifts.

We have five minutes left of our session. I know he is busy, yet I can see that something is on his mind and he hasn't raised it in our conversation so far. I have another client in 30 minutes, so I make a choice. 'Okay, well if you need to talk anything through, then give me a call. Or we can save it for next time we meet?'

'Sure.' The tone is strong. He sounds definite. We walk out of the room together talking about nothing other than plans for the weekend, the weather, the commute.

I didn't see him again. In October 2012, he took his life.

I can't pretend for one minute that a conversation with me might have made any difference at all to this lovely man and the choice he made. But I don't know. I feel profoundly troubled to this day that I was driven by my watch and didn't give him the opportunity to dig a little deeper. I didn't read the signs and I didn't know how to ask the questions.

Perhaps, having read this book, you will feel better equipped to master whatever conversations come your way.

The strategies in this book are about understanding – finding a way to understand others through listening and then finding a way to help your listeners understand you.

These are acts of kindness that will transform your leadership, and how others experience working with you.

And who knows? They may even save a life.

Every act of communication is a miracle of translation.
Ken Liu

Acknowledgements

I was lucky in the summer of 2020 to connect with Alison Jones of Practical Inspiration Publishing. Her encouragement, support, creativity and dedication to writers and writing have refreshed and inspired me, and I will be forever grateful to her for the opportunity to write this book.

I always thought writing a book must be a rather solitary activity, but I have been delighted to learn that the generosity and support of others in helping craft ideas and content, giving their time and energy in offering constructive feedback and suggestions, have made it feel like a more collaborative endeavour.

I am so grateful to the following friends and colleagues whose input and help was invaluable: Josephine Bush, Sheena Cartwright, Alan Robertson, Louise McDonald, Tamsin Vine, Grant Morffew and Andrea Tully. I'd especially like to thank Tilly Wickens, who read the manuscript first and kept me going as only she can.

Interviewing experts in their field about how and why they listen with such care has been a highlight for me, and I would like to thank them for their wisdom and generosity in sharing insights and advice: George Leigh, Emma Elgee, Denni Sayers, Andrea Ainsworth, Maggie Cameron MBE, Joanne Kearsley, Dr Rachel Mason, Dave Bourn, Ben Yeger, Damion Wonfor and Alistair Cameron.

I'm also grateful to Charlie Unwin for letting me share his three-quarter brew story.

I am blessed with many wonderful, tolerant friends who were prepared to listen to me with love and patience through periods of self-doubt and who kept me in good humour – and some wine – throughout. I would particularly like to thank my 'Road Trippers', Jules Gray, and in particular Josephine and Damien Bush and Sarah Sturt, for being my special tribe through this and at so many other times in my life.

I'd like to thank Bella Wickens for finding the patience to take my photograph… and for being my little champion in every way.

Finally, there could never be enough hours in a day, or words in the lexicon, to express my love and thanks to Russell.

CPSIA information can be obtained
at www.ICGtesting.com
Printed in the USA
JSHW032330170621
15949JS00004B/9

9 781788 602570